D1429482

PURE COLOUR

PURE COLOUR

A Pure Style Sourcebook of Colour Inspiration

JANE CUMBERBATCH

PAVILION

First published in the United Kingdom in 2015 by
Pavilion
1 Gower Street
London
WC1E 6HD

ISBN 978-1-90981-598-8

A CIP catalogue record for this book is available from the British Library.

10 9 8 7 6 5 4 3 2 1

Reproduction by Mission Productions Ltd, Hong Kong
Printed and bound by 1010 Printing International Ltd, China

Photography by Jane Cumberbatch
Design and layout by Vanessa Courtier

This book can be ordered direct from the publisher at www.pavilionbooks.com

Contents

Introduction

Pure Colour is my visual notebook of ideas and inspiration showing you how to furnish your life with colour. For ease of reading, it's divided into blues, greens, white, yellows, pinks and naturals. The book invites you to look around more closely at the everyday things in life, and it shows you how you might get inspiration from a painted café table or a beautiful ribbed shell.

Paintboxes of pure colour

The garden, the sea and landscape are my colour charts, my paintboxes of ideas and inspiration. From the green beans of the vegetable patch to the eau de Nil wash of a calm evening tide, I store these images in my head like snapshots, everyday ideas to furnish my home with freshness and simplicity. The first pink rosebud on a May morning is as perfect a shade for one of my wallpaper borders as it is a cue for my lipstick colour or the fabric for a long, swirly summer skirt.

Tissue paper petals

My love of colour began way back with pram views of sky as my mum wheeled me across the common: a baby's view of the world seen as a soaring sheet of blue with white puffy clouds. In primary school there was a craze for swapping 'diamonds' in jewel-bright colours: turquoise, emerald and ruby-coloured pieces of glass from our grandmas' remnants bags. I kept my stash nestled on cotton wool in a matchbox to be extracted carefully from my coat pocket for a sneak peak at break and to brighten the prospect of chapped knees and kiss chase. Art classes and time to make and do in a pre-Facebook age has also nurtured my passion for colour. I remember my eight-year-old production line of bright tissue-paper flowers for the school fête, and how I made my first fabric choice – red corduroy for a home-sewn skirt.

Local inspiration

I find inspiration in what's close to me and local, both in my south London garden of petals and grass shades, and in the sludge greens of the English countryside. I think about going on a family visit to the West Country, driving down the main road across the sweeping chalk contours of Salisbury Plain and past ancient Stonehenge, then descending towards a patchwork of Somerset fields in all the glittering greens of the season. And then I think about how I'd like to have a room painted in one of those greens, a way of bringing nature inside as an echo of the landscape.

Heading south for ideas

Like juxtaposition in poetry, contrast and difference is also my inspiration. Maybe it's my Caribbean heritage, or simply the need to fly south like a swallow in winter, that has made me set up house in Olhão, a small fishing town in the Portuguese Algarve. There the intense sea and sky hues, the luminosity of parched red earth in olive groves, and the butter-yellow beachscape give me limitless visual direction and a counterpoint to northern views.

Colour in art

The early twentieth-century artist Winifred Nicholson's theory of colour resonates with me. She describes colour like musical scales, the chart on which colour artists build the conceptions of their painting. She says that each colour is unique but no colour can stand alone. To get the full value of its unique colour, it must have other hues by its side. She describes a yellow posy for the table. She picked Iceland poppies, marigolds and yellow iris, but her bunch wouldn't say 'yellow'. Then she added two everlasting sweet peas in magenta pink and describes how all her yellows broke into luminosity.

Much as Nicholson's bunch lost its yellowness in all of its yellowness, I think that all-white interior schemes, for example, become clinical and dull. White only becomes fresh and alive when it is contrasted with splashes of colour – fabrics in crisp blue stripes, perhaps, to lift it out of sameness and monotony. Similarly, I will add interest to my vegetable-garden green-painted sitting room with a jug of shocking-pink roses. It's a way of making colours sing together. Nature does it so well, too – think of pink rhubarb with acid-yellow leaves.

Jane Cumberbatch

A simple colour wheel is very useful, like a visual map showing how colours relate to each other, and how they contrast and harmonize.

Yellow
Yellow-orange
Orange
Orange-red
Red
Red-violet
Violet
Violet-blue
Blue
Blue-green
Green
Yellow-green

Colour notes – helpful for understanding how colours contrast and harmonize

Primary colours

Red, yellow and blue – no colours can be mixed together to make them.

Secondary colours

Green, orange and violet – made by mixing equal parts of two primary colours.

Tertiary colours

Red-orange, red-violet, blue-violet, blue-green, yellow-green, yellow-orange – made by mixing a primary colour with its secondary neighbour.

Harmonious colours

Harmony is the effect made by using any colour together with its next neighbour or neighbours in their natural order – for example, yellow-green, green and blue-green.

How colours create contrast with their complementaries on the colour wheel

Complementary colours are any two colours that are directly opposite each other, such as orange-yellow and blue; red and green-blue; and yellow-green and violet. These opposing colours create maximum contrast and maximum stability – for example, Van Gogh said that the blueness of the sky depended on the contrast of the blue to its complementary colour, orange, and that colours could be made brilliant by contrasting each colour to its complementary. To get his Provence sky blue, Van Gogh concentrated on golden-orange cornfields and orange-red soil.

In a room, for example, you could upholster a sofa in golden-yellow and accessorize it with cushions in contrasting and complementary violet.

Colour discord

Discord is created by using colours that are widely separated on the colour wheel, such as a primary and a tertiary beyond an adjacent secondary – for example, pink and orange. Colour discord is a reversal of Rood's natural order. In large masses they are unendurable, but in small amounts they add much to brilliance and vibration. Think of a single vase of bright pink roses against a blue wall, for example. The pink breaks up the overwhelmingness of the blue and excites the eye. I suppose my lips painted in fuchsia pink lipstick are a kind of personal colour discord, definitely enlivening the overall look.

Neutral colours

Neutrals are obtained by mixing pure colours with white, black or grey, or by mixing two complementary colours. They are easily modified by adjacent, more saturated colours and they appear to take on the hue complementary to the saturated colour. Next to a bright red couch, a grey wall will appear distinctly greenish.

Monochromatic colours

Shades and tints of one colour.

Warm colours versus cool

Warm colours are said to be hues from red through yellow, browns and tans; cool colours are said to be from blue-green to blue-violet, including greys. In terms of perception, warm colours are said to advance while cool colours recede.

Achromatic colours

Any colour that lacks strong chromatic content is said to be *unsaturated, achromatic* or *near neutral*. Pure achromatic colours include black, white and all greys; near neutrals include browns, tans, pastels and darker colours. Near neutrals can be of any hue or lightness.

More about colour

Fashions in colour come and go, but I approach colour instinctively, choosing what I like because it feels right.

Without getting too bogged down in its complexities, and for physics nerds only, it is helpful to know some basics around the theory of colour: tools, as it were, for understanding why colours 'go with each other' and how opposite colours attract. It can also help you when exploring paint charts so that you don't break out in a sweat when confronted with a choice of fifty shades of everything.

Colour for real?

It's morning. The cicadas are buzzing and I've set up my workspace in a shady corner of a rented Southern Italian farmhouse. On the scrubbed wooden table there's a woven basket piled high with plump red plum tomatoes, ripe from the kitchen garden. But in truth, the tomatoes are everything but red. This is because when light hits a red tomato, only the red rays are reflected into our eyes, and we say 'red'. The other rays are absorbed. We see the rejected colour and say a tomato is red.

Edwin Land, inventor of the Polaroid Land Camera and instant photography, suggested that we judge colours by the way they relate to each other. We compare them to one another and revise, according to the time of day, light source and our memory. A tomato remains red in our minds, but think how different its red looks under electric light, or in the salad crisper.

Colour doesn't occur in the world but in the mind. The philosophical question whether or not a tree falling in the forest when no one is around makes a sound has a parallel in vision. If no human eye is around to view it, is an apple really red?

Colours exist because our minds create them as an interpretation of the electromagnetic waves that are pulsing around us. The frequency range is huge, from radio waves, which have more than 10km between them, to the tiny cosmic waves, which move in wavelengths of about a billionth of a millimetre. The human eye can detect a very small portion of this range, with wavelengths between 0.00038mm and 0.00075mm. We know this as visible light and we can distinguish about 10 million variations in it. When we see the whole range of visible light together, our eyes read it as white. When some of the wavelengths are missing, we register it as colour. Humans translate what we experience into concepts like objects, smells, sounds and colours. Most people can identify between 150 and 200 colours but we don't all see exactly the same colours, especially if we're partly or completely colour blind. Because people with albinism lack a dark layer of cells behind the retina, more light travels around their eyes and colours often seem to them quieter and more diluted.

Not all languages name all colours. Japanese only recently included a word for blue. It used to be that 'aoi' was a generic idea

that stood for the range of colours from green and blue to violet. In Swahili, 'nyajund'u' could mean brown, yellow, grey or green.

The vision problems of some artists illustrates how we all 'see' differently. Mark Twain described Turner's later paintings as like a ginger cat having a fit in a bowl of tomatoes; Turner was short-sighted, which causes reds to be more defined. And after Monet's cataracts were treated, he was surprised by all the blueness in things and retouched the strange colours of his recent work.

Nature and colour

Stretched out under the beach umbrella on a bleached blue summer's day, it seems appropriate to be reading up on the colour theory of late nineteenth-century physicist Ogden Rood. He was keen on the idea of a natural order of colours, as they are in the spectrum, going from yellow, which is the lightest of colours, to violet, the darkest, and that one may go between these extremes by two roads, by way of red or by way of blue. The natural order is for orange to be deeper than yellow, red deeper than orange and so on down to violet. Similarly green is deeper than yellow, blue deeper than green, and violet deeper than blue. Rood describes looking at a sunset for following the natural order

of colours: yellow turning to orange, orange to red, red to crimson and crimson to purple. In the case of trees, the young foliage is light and yellowish, then changes to green with a deepening of colour. In autumn, when turning yellow, the foliage becomes lighter. In nasturtiums, for instance, when red and yellow come together, the red will be the darker, while crimson will be darker than red. Fruits follow the natural order too. Oranges and lemons, green at first, become lighter as they become yellower; melons, pumpkins and vegetable marrows do the same.

Inspiration 1

I'm as besotted with my garden as the bees are sated on sweet nectar from the starry alliums. It feels almost electric with activity: bursting, glossy pink roses, voluptuous peonies shedding brilliant carpets of petals, and crowds of bees, enough, if there were such a thing, for a bee club night.

Summer-garden colours and rose-petal pinks

I get up close, eye to bee pollen sac; there are black-and-white striped ones, fat yellow ones, small bobbly, hairy ones, and brown fluffy types as if they'd had a cut and blow dry.

NB Purples and pinks are the most vibrant of colours to go with the greens of the garden – very lovely too on fabrics.

Inspiration 2

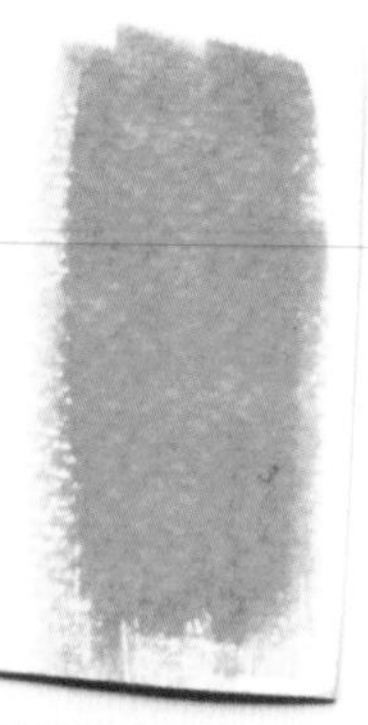

Olhão colour

As I pack away t-shirts and cool dresses at the end of the holidays, it's one thing to have visual records of Olhão's unmanicured charm, but another to convey the pot-pourri of smells: overworked drains, rotting fish, the waft of a honeysuckle in a hidden courtyard; beery fisherman, lingering herb cologne, home-cooked stews, the ozone and saltness of the sea air. They're so evocative of the place, it's hard to conjure them up mentally, but London suburban street air seems so bland in comparison, even when the foxes have been having a party by the dustbins.

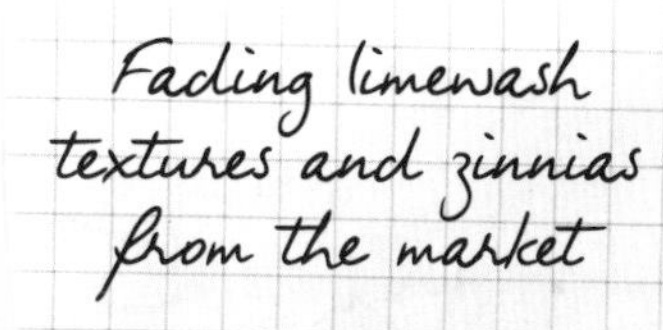

Inspiration 3

Landscape greens

The patchwork of greens, blues, greys, yellows and earth reds are part of what's wild and beautiful about the English landscape. I take the greens of the downs and limpid-blue spring skies

into the house and use them in abundance. These colours are as easy on the eye and mind as they are when drinking in their pleasures on a summer cliff walk or hike through the English Norfolk fields.

Apples, quinces and all the golden corn colours at the end of summer are ripe inspiration for paint shades. And versatile, too: yellows go so well with blues and other more surprising partners, such as purple.

Of sea, sky and hyacinths

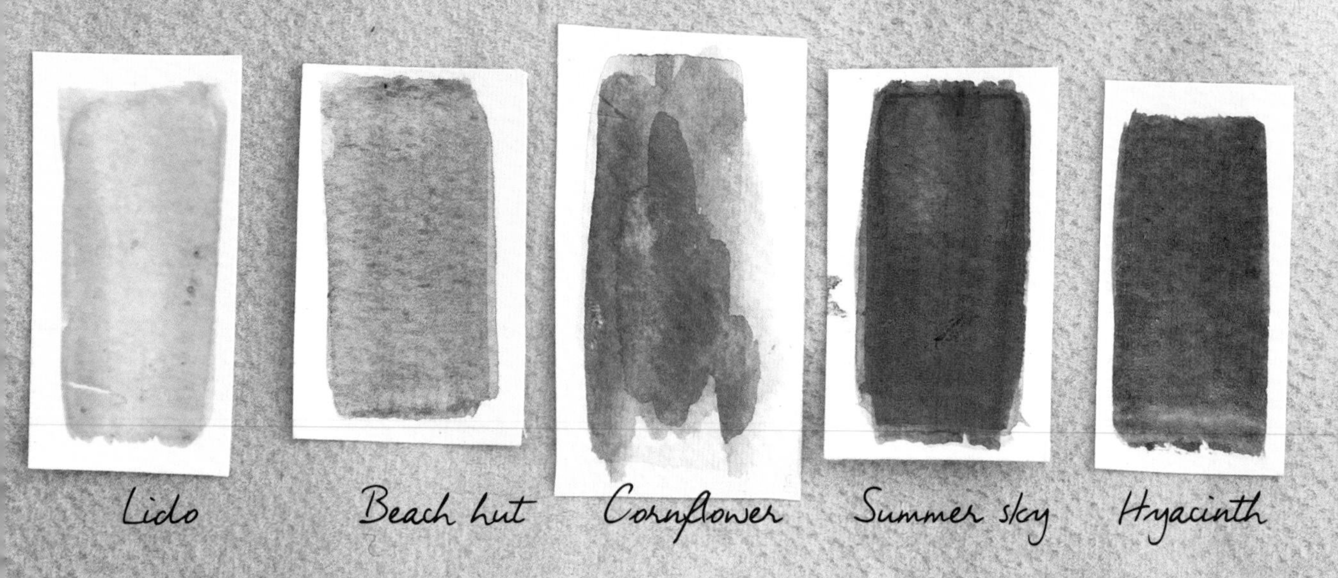

I am lying on the beach. Pinpricks of sun flicker through the straw hat protecting my face and there is the gentle swish of the incoming tide. I'm thinking blue – a blue brainstorm, as it were. Washed in endless blue, the sky is for starters, then soft cobalt limewashed walls baked and warm in the sun at the beach house on the Portuguese island of Culatra. I remember Howard Hodgkin's giant blue wave mural in tiles at the sports club where I once attempted to keep fit. But the blues have to be at their most intense in Matisse's cut-outs at London's Tate Modern. I think about home and the kitchen shelves spread with blue-and-white tartan china, bought from Anta the tartan specialist, and the dependable blue-and-white striped ticking cotton on chairs all over the house. In Olhão, there is a haze of lavender-blue agapanthus in the courtyard, while white linen tea towels with a deep-blue stripe toast on the washing line.

Gracias por su visita
Telem. 917 634 813 - 8700 OLHÃO
BILHETE SÓ IDA
OLHÃO - CULATRA - OLHÃO
Nº 33740
AMEIJOA BOA
31/08/2013
LAS LEGÍTIMAS Y ACREDITADAS
TORTAS DE ACEITE
DE
INES ROSALES
CALLE REAL, 102

I do like the uniformity of a smart blue-and-white stripe. It may have something to do with the fact that in summer my mum dressed my sister and me in matching blue striped sailor shirts and blue cotton shorts – they represented the holidays, the end of school and ice creams from the van. A nervous child, as I was, I appreciated order and, in their way, the striped shirts, cotton shorts and shifts, and sensible sandals were symbols of comfort routine. Good feelings about the colour blue have continued to resonate with me over the decades.

Beach cool in Puglia
on an Italian holiday:
blue canvas wooden
recliners with shade
attachments

Going south with rich cobalt blues

Painter Piers de Laszlo has made it his life's work to prop up and furnish Olhão's elegant and faded interiors – a collector and curator of needy houses, you could say. He has a very good way with blue pigment, sometimes using it as a pale wash on courtyard walls, and then – as here in his 'blue' house – going for a really deep-blue look. Piers mixes the powder with water and builder's glue to bind it and give adhering power. In the past, this colour originally came from natural ultramarine, made from lapis lazuli. Artificial ultramarine appeared in the nineteenth century, together with cobalt blue.

Dapple shade and blue Spanish tiles on a hot summer afternoon in a palm-tree-fringed Ayamonte plaza

Harmony and contrast: paler shades of blue-and-green check upholstery in a winged armchair work well with the rich cobalt-blue background

Tough cotton canvas umbrellas are more expensive but superior in quality. I have learnt that it's a false economy to buy flimsy nylon versions; they seem to collapse inside out and fail by the end of week one of the holiday at most.

Olhão bar chic

Blue limewash walls and pavement furniture in lime green and complementary orange shades.

On beach trips, I travel light with hammam woven towels (the ones used in Turkish hammam baths), which double as a picnic blanket, towel, sarong and even a windbreak when needed. The great thing is that they are light but very absorbent and they dry quickly.

Something for the outdoors in blue-and-white cotton

Under the apple tree in my garden there's an old school table I bought for a fiver from a charity shop. When it's warm enough to eat outside or to have a mug of tea and a slice of cake in the dappled shade of the afternoon, I dress up the table with a cloth. It might be the blue-and-white striped one made from four linen tea towels sewn together, or the chambray denim-coloured one with a simple *Little House on the Prairie*-style frilled edge, and then there's always something from my thick pile of blue-and-white checks.

Notes on blue

Beach scene at Camber Sands

Family heirloom: blue patchwork with remnants of the children's jeans

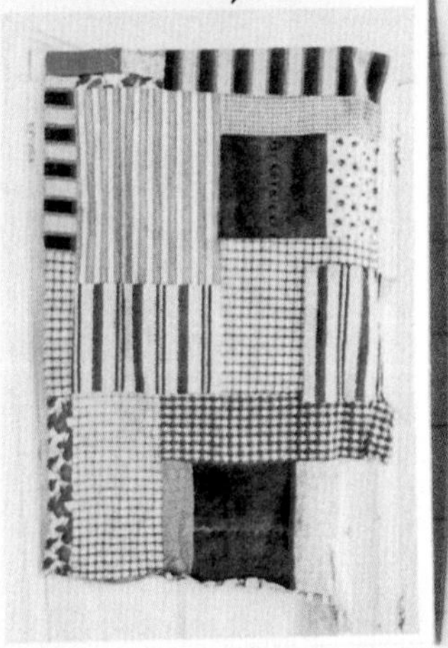

In his Theory of Colours (1810), the German poet, artist and politician, Johann Wolfgang von Goethe, wrote that 'there is something contradictory in blue's aspect, both stimulating and calming. Just as we wish to pursue a pleasant object that moves away from us, we enjoy gazing upon blue – not because it forces itself upon us but because it draws us after it.' Blue represents transcendence at one level, hence the medieval paintings with the Virgin Mary swathed in blue, and on another, the blues of depression and low mood.

Why the sky is blue

In the earth's atmosphere, blue appears from lightest azure to the deepest blue-black of the night sky. The nineteenth-century physicist, John Tyndall, used the sea as a way of explaining the colour of the sky. If waves crash against a tall cliff, they would stop; if they meet a rock, only the smaller waves are affected; whereas a pebble will change the course of only the tiniest waves washing against the beach. This is what happens with light from the sun. The largest wavelengths, the red ones, are mainly unaffected, and it is only the smallest ones, the blue and violet ones, which are scattered by molecules in the the sky, giving the eye the sensation of blue.

Blue jeans

Pure blue is a colour containing no trace of yellow or red. On the colour spectrum, it lies between blue-green and blue-violet, or indigo, as it is also known.

The colour indigo, from the Greek term meaning 'from India', has a complete history and story of its own. Derived from the plant of the same name, and also from woad, indigo has been used for thousands of years as a dye, paint and a medicine. Egyptian mummies were wrapped in indigo-dyed cloths; the ancient Britons daubed themselves in woad. The British East India Company began shipping indigo to Europe from the seventeenth century.

In mid-nineteenth century America, businessman Levi Strauss spotted a gap in the market for tough workwear, and imported indigo-dyed cloth from Nîmes in France, called 'serge de Nimes' or denim as it became known. Later, the trousers were named jeans, after the Genoese sailors who transported the cloth. English dyers used to classify many shades of indigo with elegant descriptions such as milk blue, pearl blue, pale blue, flat blue, middling, sky blue, queen's blue, watchet blue, garter blue, mazareen blue, deep blue and navy blue.

On a trip to Guilin in China in the mid 1980s, I remember weaving my way through a surge of indigo blue as I went through the market. Shrunken women with lined faces and buns knotted at the nape of their necks, old men with long pipes, children with the customary trousers open to the elements – everyone was kitted out in indigo-coloured, Mao-style cotton tops and bottoms. The only other colour among the charcoal braziers, dumplings rising under cloths, and makeshift stalls covered with more blue awnings, was the wool seller, whose skeins of bright pink, green and blue seemed almost electric in contrast.

Retro blue and white

Blue rooms

The general notion is that rooms decorated in blue will appear larger, as blue has the effect of making spaces recede. The warm, dark blues lie towards the red part of the spectrum and the cooler blues towards green. A brilliant use of indigo can be seen at Seville airport, where its cathedral-like proportions soar to a beautiful, glowing, indigo-coloured ceiling that has the rich textures of an Andalucian night sky.

Lighter warm blues work all over the house, and can also be mixed with limewash to decorate exterior walls and outdoor patios in seaside settings such as Olhão, where the good light makes the colour more enriched and luminous. These blues work well with complementary oranges and greys, yellow, reds and lavender.

Although deep, cool blues were used by Picasso during his 'blue period' to create moody, introspective themes; it is said that he was actually depressed during his pink period. Whenever I have felt low, I would say that blue is a rather comforting colour to be around and, of course, it is redolent of the sea and sky, the better things in life.

Grey-blues or green-blues are the ones I like most of all for their light-enhancing qualities. They are understated, allowing one to play with contrasting colour, such as splashes of pink, and natural wood and stone textures. These colours suit our northern climate so well.

Swatch box blues

Liberty, Fresco, Nesfield Collection, linen/cotton mix

Vintage Laura Ashley cotton from my fabric box

THE NESFIELD FABRICS ©

polka dot cotton from my fabric box

MacCulloch & Wallis, Macgingham in Turquoise, cotton

Liberty Print in Pepper, in tana lawn

Romo, Linara in Agapanthus, cotton/linen mix

Les Indiennes Reverse Coeur, cotton

Rapture and Wright, Hopscotch in Chinese Green Comp, linen union

Romo, Orchis in Kanoko Delft, linen/cotton

Mark Alexander, Haven 1, Peaceful Inidigo linen
Les Indiennes, Lucie in Indigo, cotton
The Art of Wallpaper, 3in stripe, wallpaper
Osborne and Little, Lorca, Louisiane, cotton
Olicana, Orkney in Multi Blue, cotton
Vintage Laura Ashley cotton from a fabric box
Mini Moderns, Darjeeling wallpaper in Chalkhill Blue
Louise Body, Paper Tile Collection in Old Blue

Blue-and-white striped cotton ticking covers are the little black dresses of the chair scene

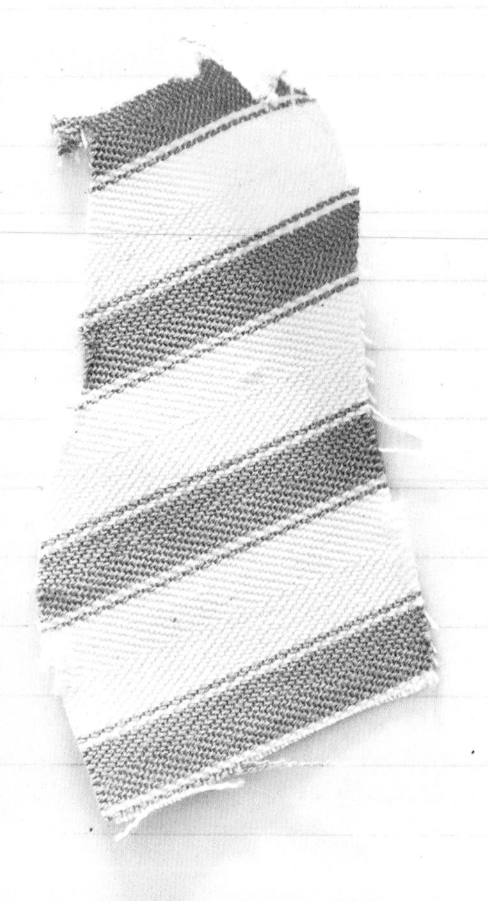

Vintage schoolroom cupboards are painted in the same brilliant white as the walls, but substituting emulsion for an acrylic eggshell finish. This gives a clean, uncluttered canvas, as do the floorboards, painted in a tough white floor paint.

The woven cotton ticking loose covers in blue-and-white stripes can now sing out against their monochrome setting. (They also have the advantage that they can be tossed in the washing machine when they have been used and abused by muddy dog paws.)

The narrow blue-and-white stripe is easy on the eye and not in the least bit overpowering. It is left to the broad, bold, darker blue-and-white striped cushion on the armchair to give the whole look some more punch – as well as giving the sitter some comfortable back support.

White walls make the perfect backdrop for a crisp, light and bright, blue-and-white coastal feel

I paint the north-facing room with
the old wooden dresser in a quiet blue hue
that seems to speak of soft
English spring mornings

As soon as I set on the table a vase with catkins from a country walk and a bunch of sweet-scented blue hyancinths, there's a feeling of life. The spring greens and blues feel fresh, and the white-painted table and chairs help the light and airy look.

Blue, green and white spring details

Painting the floor white

On a wet day in April it may seem impractical to have painted white floors when everyone from the cat to the people on photographic shoots literally leave their mark. I don't flinch because I have a very able mop and bucket and I use Flortred floor paint that is incredibly tough and resists all but the most careless furniture shifter.

When we moved to the house, the floors were in good condition, so all that was necessary was to sand, undercoat and finish with two top coats. The paint takes a couple of days to harden completely, as it is almost like an enamel. Once a year, I repaint the floors that have the most traffic.

Pancakes + Chanel nail polish for tea
(From Dan Lepard in The Guardian.)
150g caster sugar, finely grated zest of 3 lemons, 150g soft goat's cheese, 3 large eggs + 2 extra yolks, 50g creme fraiche, 200ml lemon juice, 1x 18cm shortcrust base, blind baked + kept in tin
Beat sugar, zest and cheese until smooth.
Whisk in eggs & creme fraiche
Stir in lemon juice
Check the tart for cracks and if any brush with egg white and give a hot blast in oven to set it and give a waterproof effect.
Heat
to 170c | 33 F | gas 3
Put
tray, transfer to
Bake for
Serve cold

Blue-and-white china is a timeless fixture in the kitchen

I pick up odd plates and bowls from here, there and everywhere, in charity shops and car boot sales. Sailor-stripe Cornishware is another retro find to look out for. It was made with a lathe-turning technique that scraped blue slip away to reveal white bands of clay beneath. Made from 1926 by TG Green, the Derbyshire-based company couldn't compete with modern mass production and it closed in 2007. An enterprising team relaunched the company recently and so the familiar blue-and-white striped ceramics are available again. I prefer the slightly worn patina of the originals.

BRE
R.MUTT
FIZZ
1
tea by the sea

Kitchen blues

When artist Mandy Bonnell isn't tending her garden, she could be stirring a bubbling pan of quince jelly in her snug, 1950s-style, blue-and-turquoise basement kitchen. 'The tree is only seven years old but I got 9kg of fruit this summer.'

Some pieces, including a vintage gas cooker, a tall cabinet and the sideboard seen here, have been handed down from friends. London's Bermondsey market across the road has been a good source of retro kitchen bits and pieces. The nautical tea cosy is from Poppy Trefey in Cornwall. Mandy also staggered home across the Atlantic with a blue enamel, US fleamarket-find bread bin wrapped in a sweater in hand luggage just because she liked it so much.

Inexpensive and utilitarian kitchen kit in cool blue colours

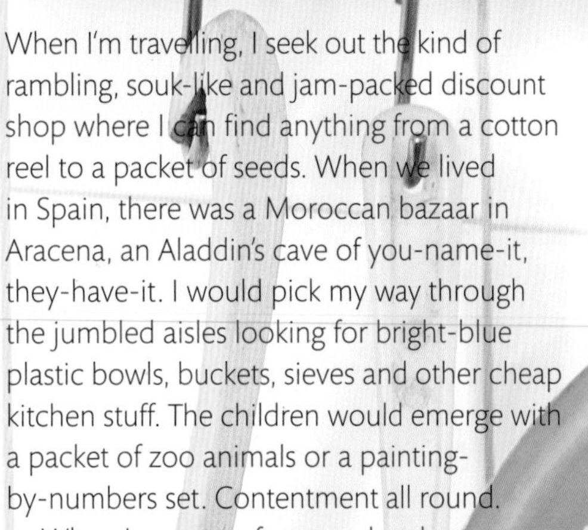

When I'm travelling, I seek out the kind of rambling, souk-like and jam-packed discount shop where I can find anything from a cotton reel to a packet of seeds. When we lived in Spain, there was a Moroccan bazaar in Aracena, an Aladdin's cave of you-name-it, they-have-it. I would pick my way through the jumbled aisles looking for bright-blue plastic bowls, buckets, sieves and other cheap kitchen stuff. The children would emerge with a packet of zoo animals or a painting-by-numbers set. Contentment all round.

When I run out of pegs or brushes and potato peelers, I cycle to Brixton and the covered market, the rough-around-the-edges part that is holding off the invasion of foodie shops and eateries.

Another use for using washing-up bowls; displays of plump olives in the market at Olhão

Street details in Olhão that could be the blues and yellows of Van Gogh's sky and cornfields

The elements may be unforgiving on the outside but a burst of painterly blue and yellow will elevate Saturday morning with the newspapers

I save the last shocking-pink rosebud from a bunch brought by a friend and put it in a small blue cup of water. In the words of mid-twentieth-century educator, florist and author, Constance Spry I feel like 'a millionaire for a few pence.'

Hippy handmade blues

Simple wall prints are easy to achieve using a sponge or potato halves cut into simple geometric shapes to make homemade stamps. Dip them in water-based paint and print your pattern across the wall, filling up with more colour as you go. I discovered the most beautiful handblocked paper on a trip to Venice nearly 30 years ago. I bought a linen-bound, flower-printed folder as a reminder of the trip and as inspiration for filling it with design cuttings. It's good to know the same shop is still tucked away in a canal-side piazza, and the folder is in my office as a continuing visual touchstone of ideas.

See far left: Indian handblocked cottons in deep indigo colours are great for recreating laid-back, 1970s-style outdoor furnishings. Think squashy bolsters and oversized cushions for chilling in the garden on a hot summer day.

Washing with blue and white, petals and cork textures

Ever keen to bring the sense of being in the countryside or by the sea into our London home, I lined the bathroom walls in tongue and grooved panels to get a homespun, cabin effect. The board is waterproofed and we used oil-based eggshell for more water resistance. The bath, a very ordinary stainless steel one, was already boxed in.

A blue-and-white blind is made from a linen teatowel gathered on linen tape and secured at hooks either side of the window frame. A slatted folding chair, painted bright blue, looks as if it could have just come back from a day trip to the beach.

Sleeping with white linen and blue pyjama stripes

Interior decorator and art director, Katrin Cargill, is famous for the way she decorates with red and white, but she is also a dab hand at blue, as seen here in the crisp blue-and-white bedroom at her home in London.

The key feature is a majestic padded headboard to Katrin's design covered in blue handblocked cotton. Headboards are a very good way of making plain divans and the surrounding walls look much more interesting.

I haven't found them yet, but my plan is to luxuriate in pure-white linen sheets edged with a simple blue stripe

After the joys of thundering down the main road west out of London, and in need of fresh air and optimism before visiting the nursing home where my father lives, I walk with the dog around the ancient woodlands at Lytes Cary, a medieval National Trust house in Somerset. There is also a large community garden there: a year-round visual treat and an example of how quite disparate plots – from basic potatoes and cabbages only to pocket versions of intricate cottage gardens – come together in a patchwork of seamless beauty.

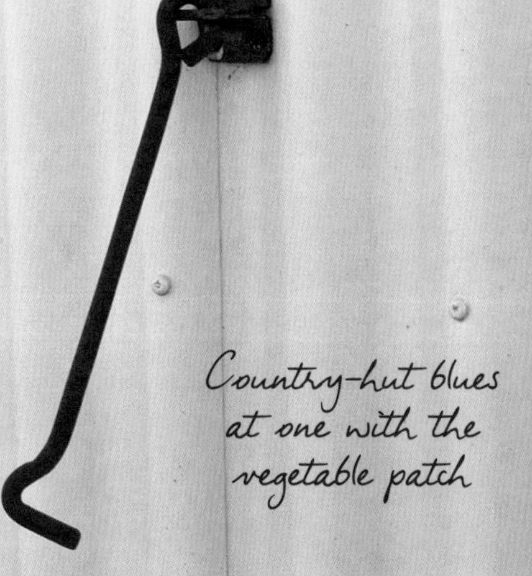

Country-hut blues at one with the vegetable patch

Over in a sheltered corner, there's a communal shed, a shepherd hut on wheels. Originally designed as mobile shelter for shepherds guarding flocks and nursing sick lambs on cold nights, traditional shepherd huts were a crucial part of Britain's agricultural history. Now they come with all mod cons and are a fixture of the glamping look.

Forget-me-not blues and other petals for simple living

A pot of Grape Hyacinths

A giant! – 'Gladiator' allium

Agapanthus in the patio Olhao

Scillas for Spring

Delphiniums

Delicate china-blue scillas mark the beginning of spring in the garden, and for the price of a bus fare, a pot of grape hyacinths gives pleasure for three weeks or more. In summer, the purply-blue alliums and thistles are magnets for the bees.

Winter + Spring hyacinth colours

Grass green and garden cabbages

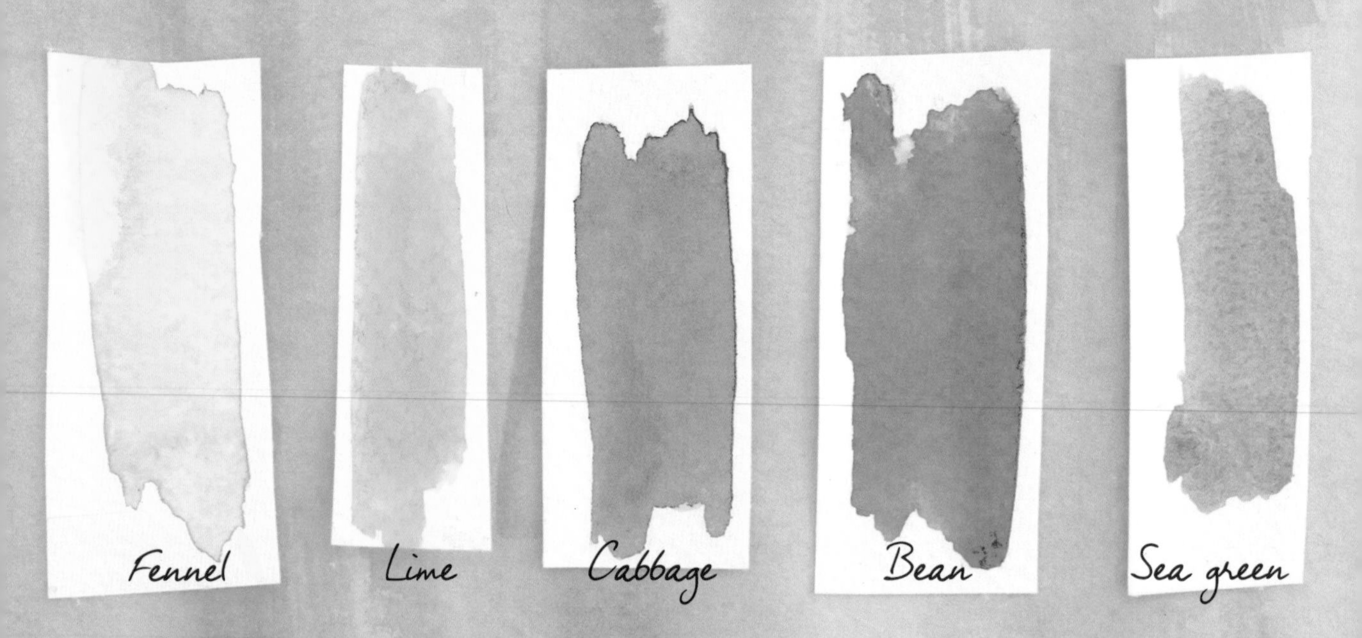

I was listening to a radio programme about books, and apparently green is the least favoured colour by publishers for covers. It has something to do with the fact that green doesn't sell itself on the shelf in the way that a brash red or an electric yellow does. And, yes indeed, greens are what makes the landscape soothing to the eye. Rich grey-greens of olives or a field in winter are timeless and quiet. And then there is the 'green' room where performers calm themselves before going on stage.

Having said this, greens do have shouty qualities at the light, bright end of the green spectrum The acidic lime greens of hyacinth stalks in spring would surely bring on an attack of nausea if splashed all around a room. But used sparingly, a shot of lime green in cushions or a bowl of green apples is a visual pep up.

Lettuce
Cabbage
Thyme
Modern Decoration
AIR-INDIA
Class Boarding Pass
ROWN/JANEMS
ONDON LHR
EW YORK JFK
W 14JUL1315
60 INCH/150 CM
1 INCH
3
Broadbean, pea + puy lentil salad – a perfect summer idea
happy Christmas
Emma Douglas

Updates and market greens

The sun is going down and bathing the fields in golden light. I'm in Somerset, podding broad beans in my sister Sarah's garden. A hen waddles across the grass and Poppadom, the cat, plays tightrope walker along the post-and-rail fence. There is something savoury and meaty on the barbecue. It's good being in the country when the weather is kind.

I like Sarah's idea of updating 1930s' Lloyd Loom basketweave chairs that have seen better days with fresh, country-garden green paint, and pairing them with pinky-red check cotton cushions – a good example of complementary colours working together and looking at one in their rural setting.

The possibilities for visual inspiration in a market are endless. I hand over a couple of notes for a hand-dyed and heating-bill-reducing, retro, green, recycled wool blanket from the Sunday stall Blankets and Ballgowns in Herne Hill. On a sailor suit-coloured morning in Olhão, I see paint-chart possibilities in glossy sheaves of grass for making herbal tea, and bright woven baskets in sea-green and white piled with snails.

I am drawn to blue-greens because they seem to me to be more of the sea and water than sky or landscape. I daydream of green-flecked white surf or calm turquoise pools and lagoons. (Read Jean Rhys's *Wide Sargasso Sea* for inspiration.) I enjoy the serendipity of coming across the same sea colour cues in an Italian church railing or painted metal café table at the bar in the square. Back home, I remember these visual snippets, positives against the negative of drab Norwood High Street in the rain.

Artist Mandy Bonnell is very good at growing a microcosm of nature's delights in her handkerchief-sized city garden. She is resourceful, too, planting up herbs and agapanthus in recycled wave-spume-coloured buckets and bins.

Daydreaming of green-flecked white surf
and turquoise pools

Arsenic hits the spot as the name for this verdigris emulsion. This bright, but not overpowering, green-blue works as well in the kitchen of a traditional Greek island whitewashed house, say, as it does in an English cottage or city studio.

Kitchen greens

A plate of delicate spaghettini tossed with cherry tomatoes, chilli and basil leaves almost shimmered against the neutral browns and whites at London's Boca di Lupo restaurant (the Italian flavour of the month) on a recent birthday outing. In plain, simple surroundings, good food will speak for itself. It reminded me that soft green, with its feel of the vegetable garden, is another food-friendly background colour that enhances rather than detracts from all that goes on in the kitchen or dining room. In sunlight, the colour is light and fresh, and at night it takes on a richer green tone.

Garden greens

The way to fill up a garden space, terrace, patio or window sill with flowers and herbs is not necessarily to buy the more expensive and mature plants. Last summer I needed to replace some lavenders that had not flourished. I bought small plug plants that were very inexpensive, and a year on they are a healthy size and flowering well. Sowing packets of annual seeds is a brilliant way for more instant colour and greenery. Nasturtiums need little encouragement and by the end of the summer will be flowing prettily over a balcony wall or fence you want to hide, and supplying flowers for the table – and salads, too. Architectural cardoons, fennel and dill plants put up lots of height very quickly – you only need one or two to make a difference in a small space.

Lime-green and silvery-grey greens for useful and beautiful herbs

Bay Dark-green glossy leaves grow into bushes (slowly) or can be trimmed into simple topiary balls. Good for flavouring meat sauces, or using in stuffing for chicken.

Chives Fluffy purple flowers and bright-green stems from the allium family, chives make good front-of-border decoration. Chop the onion-flavoured stems for garnishes in soups and salads. The flowers are edible, too.

Fennel Good for height (1.5m/5ft) with feathery green leaves and delicate yellow flower spikes. I use the leaves to flavour fish. I don't grow it for the bulb.

Lavender In high summer, the lavender spills over the paths in a mass of silver and grey-green leaves and purple-blue flower spikes. The dog returns to her basket smelling like a scent shop. Try a salad served on a bed of rocket and lavender sprigs.

Lemon balm Rampant but pretty lime-green leaves that I cut into ball shapes to keep in check. I add it to flower posies and use it for herbal tea, salads, to stuff fish and to decorate a summery pudding of meringues and cream.

Oregano and marjoram With similar habits, these herbs tend to be sprawling if left to grow, but have pretty, delicate leaves. I use both to flavour tomato salads, to stuff roast birds, and for sauces.

Rocket Excellent for bright green, low-level detail (cut it regularly to stop it going to seed and looking gangly – although the yellow flowers are attractive). One packet sown directly into the ground in early summer produces a continual supply of bitter, peppery leaves for salads.

Rosemary Glossy grey-green, spiked leaves grow into substantial bushes if south facing (my north-facing ones are half the size). I use sprigs of rosemary for making Christmas wreaths and to flavour roast lamb, chicken, potatoes and fish.

Sage With silvery grey-green or variegated leaves, sage is an evergreen perennial that is available in many varieties. The herb is great with fried eggs, pasta and risotto.

Thyme A lowish-growing herb with small leaves, thyme can be trimmed into neat, textural clumps. Lemon thyme is my favourite; I use it to decorate roast meats and fish.

Edible greens

Rocket, basil, mozarella
olive oil: perfect summer
salad

I fill up my shopping bag with glee when floppy-headed savoy cabbages, with their extraordinary deep-veined leaf detail, are in the market. It's a no-brainer: eat up your greens!

Lightly steamed and seasoned
with butter, lemon and garlic,
a plate of greens is such a
simple, inexpensive way to eat
something that looks so pretty
and is so good for you

Notes on the garden

Cottage-garden inspiration

Spring colour at Rosendal organic garden, Stockholm

Just as a sunlit room decorated with honey-coloured tiles can lend support to whatever is most hopeful in us, so can the garden on a still, blue, summer's day. My garden landscape is like an old-fashioned floral fabric print of blousy pink and purple buds and blooms against light, bright summer greens.

I am inspired by the traditional cottage garden with its combination of ornamental and useful elements. I have divided half the garden into 16 potager-style beds, which are planted with a mixture of edible herbs and, in the centre, four standard roses which give the space a sense of height. Gravel paths divide each bed, and at either end of the central path there is a simple Gothic, grey-metal trellised arch, which supports old-fashioned, scented sweet peas.

Shrub roses border the garden on the left and right, and in summer they are a riot of pink and white blooms. Then there is a patch of grass, which I leave long and meadow-like, and the apple tree, spreading its leafy canopy to create shade for outdoor feasts.

I painted the 1930s' garden shed in a soft, pale blue-green to make it blend in with the plant and leaf colours, and the fencing is washed with blue-green water-based paint that also ties the whole look together.

Greens and pinks and purples ...

The first pink tulip of spring is always an excitement, with its hopeful splash of colour against the fresh new greening. I plant tulips sparingly among the beds because it gives the eye a chance to appreciate each stem, and it also creates a simple, airy look to the space.

Then the alliums stretch skywards and shimmer and fizz in purple brilliance: edible pompoms for every bee in the neighbourhood.

Alliums in full bloom

Over summer, the cardoon plant spreads its large silvery-green leaves and grows to nearly 2m/6ft, with bright blue flowers like a thistle on steroids. And there is more spreading, delicate, purple detail in the verbena plants, which are just as beautiful when they dry out in autumn

Light in the garden

My garden has moods and textures that change with the time of day, the quality of light, and whatever the elements are supplying.

In the way that south-facing rooms are glaring and uncomfortable in full sunlight, so the garden is bleached and distant at noon in July when I choose to retreat to the cool of my bedroom. But later, after Earl Grey and a chocolate bar, the garden is suffused with pleasing light and shade; roses curl and unfurl in a siesta of translucent languorous petals; long, low sunbeams track the green gloss finish of the garden furniture, and the bees dangle and dodge along the rays as if on a highway in the air.

On the other hand, the dullest no-show-of-sun day gives the garden a rather wonderful, saturated matt quality, like in a David Hockney landscape.

All the colours and textures of leaves and petals seem to advance and intensify against the grey canvas of sky. And after a rainstorm, with all the petals and leaves washed clean and dripping, the garden is all bright and refreshed greens in the drying sunlight.

Summer eating under the apple tree

Green and purple in my summer garden

Purple hyacinths and Neisha Crosland wallpaper: a fabulous combination in my friend Clare's hallway

Vintage and modern florals

Going through the fabric cupboard on the landing, I come across a chair cover in a vintage Colefax and Fowler floral print of rambling and delicate geraniums. It seems to echo the pink, white and purple scented sweet peas I grew from seed, which curl around the grey metal trellised arches in the garden. I think the pattern looks fresh and modern against bright-pink Nancy's Blushes emulsion.

I bought a sack of old BBC costumes from a junk shop for the children's dressing-up box and among frayed net petticoats and peasant shirts there was a jolly 1950s' pink and green, rosebud-printed apron. I couldn't resist chopping it up for sewing projects, including a patch to decorate my daughter's jeans.

Swatch box greens

Oceana, Baltic in Royal Fern, cotton
Les Indiennes, Fleur in Olive, Cotton
Penny Morrison Fabrics, Anya in Green, linen
Osborne & Little, Santorini, Ikaria, linen/polyester mix
Pure Style border, Fennel
John Lewis, Henley Check in Sage, cotton
MissPrint, Little Trees in Moss, linen/cotton/nylon mix

Whether it's bud, stem or fabric detailing, a splash of lime green will look good with blue-green and white, and as a brilliant contrast to pink

The photographic shoots often come laden with tempting fabrics, furniture and other props and I get the feeling that it would be good to throw out all my stuff and start again. Lime-green Habitat chairs inspire me to paint a junk chair for the office in a bright Dulux lime green. And so the recycling of ideas goes on as other shoots use it in their pictures too.

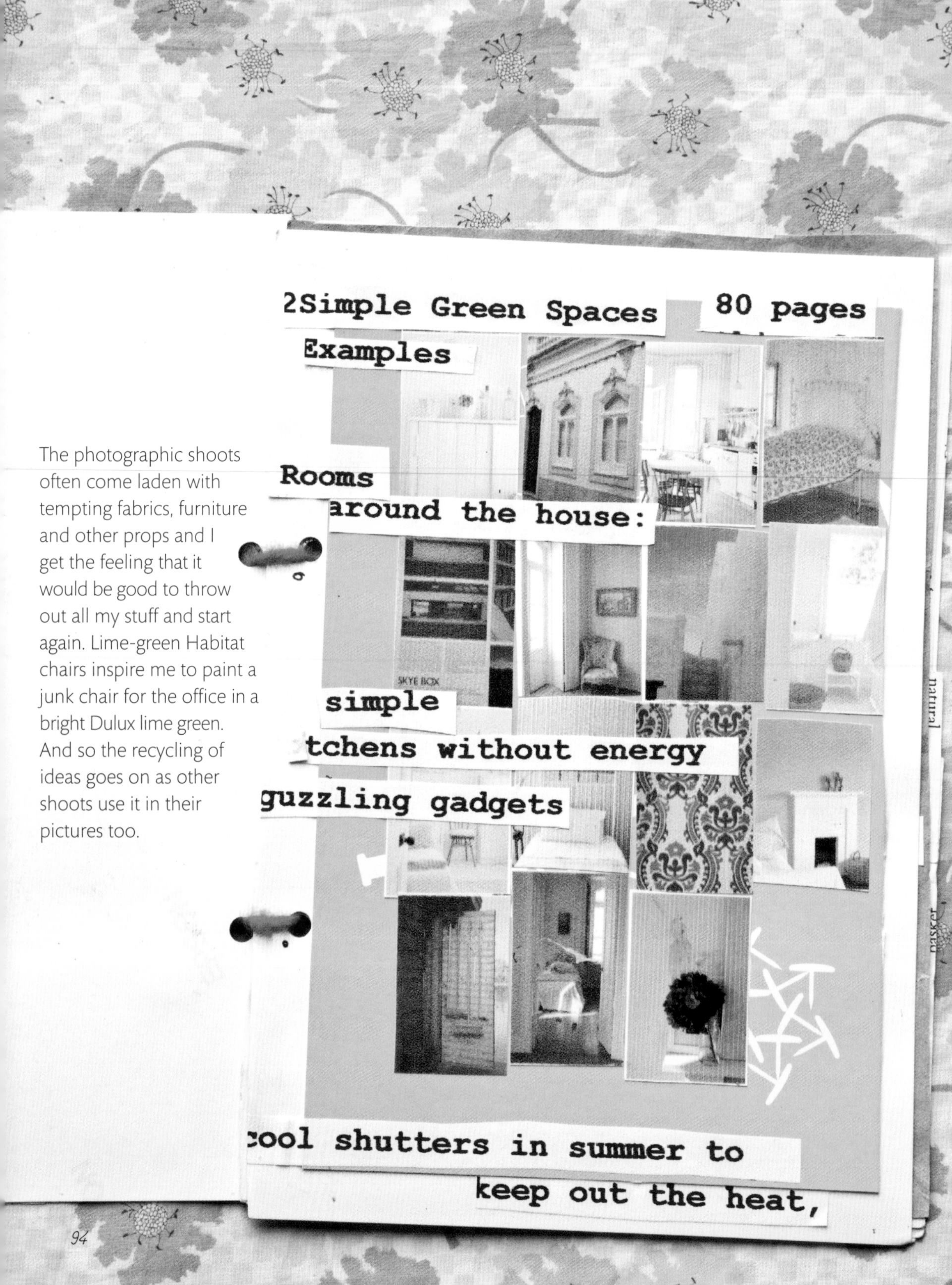

Like a magpie I gather images and thoughts, in notebooks (like this one on green and eco ideas) and on the big painted cork noticeboard in the office.

The tree is laden with its glossy green crop of cooking apples. As well as apple cake for tea, there's the visual pleasure of garden greens in a simple white bowl on the table.

Together with crocheted loo roll holders and nylon sheets, it is good that the avocado-coloured bathroom died out with the 1970s. Photographer Jo Tyler likes green, but the bathroom at her house in a very popular location in South London is in a rich olive colour, the new avocado, one might say. The luminous green Moroccan tiles by Habibi give it a calm and relaxing Ihaman feel. Resourceful Jo found the bath on eBay; the feet were rescued from a muddy field at her family's farm. The bath panel is painted with blackboard paint, which knocks it into the background and directs the eye towards the calming water.

Luminous green tiles inspired by the hammam

This is Citrine, a strong green that resonates with the greens and earth colours of the garden. The paint chart notes that it was used in the 1950s and recommends it for a north-facing room with a pale greeny-yellow and a chocolate brown. It's also a good colour to go with sludgy blues and has enough yellow in it to keep it rich and warm.

In autumn, I bring nature inside with pumpkins, quinces, red onions and pomegranates on the table to create that harvest-home look. When my children were small, we'd press leaves in scrapbooks – a simple way to make decorations, too.

In autumn, landscape greens meld with golden leaf and natural earth colours

No
trespassing

Clouds, cool patios, crisp white sheets

Some people think that all-white houses are cold and unwelcoming. They can be, particularly the sharp-edged, uptight minimalist type where there is not a sign of real life because its hidden away behind cleverly disguised white fixtures and fittings. White works when it's combined with natural textures that play to its whiteness and give it life.

Gracias por su visita
CHESTNUT PUREE TART
4 oz butter, + 2 tbps
butter for mould 4 eggs
separated, 1 Vanilla pod,
2 tbsp orange zest, 16 oz
sweet chestnut purée,
2 tbps selfraising flour
Pinch of salt, 1/4 cup
creme fraiche, 1 tbps
icing sugar for decoration
– METHOD –
CRITIC

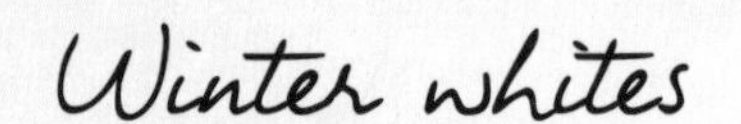

It is a release to peel off wool layers and sunbathe under a blue sky busy with swallows, tweeting sparrows and swooping nets of silvery homing pigeons. We go to the Saturday market in Olhão and load the Rolly Rolser shopping trolley on wheels with an armful of flowers, local eggs, wild asparagus and oranges.

Clumps of grass between cobbles and strange weeds sprouting on terracotta pantiled roofs show why Olhão in winter does as good a trade in wellington boots as the local chain store in Brixton. The difference, though, in going south is that the light is bright and energising all year round, and the white limewashed walls at the house make it summery even in February.

If a space is all white, with everything in it white, then it could only be too clinical, too relentless on the eye and the spirit. So without detracting from its light and space-enhancing qualities, I balance the look with natural textures: rough terracotta floor tiles, a wooden table made from reclaimed and sun-bleached floorboards, and simple wooden seating.

Note the Scandi connection between the white lanterns I buy by the boxful from Ikea and simple white wooden detail on one of the houses at Skansen Open Air Museum of traditional Swedish buildings in Stockholm

Limewash creates a soft matt finish that gives the walls a textured organic look. The way it weathers, too, is so much part of limewash's appeal. Limewash has practical advantages in that it allows the surface it covers to breathe. If you intend to make your own, it is safest to use lime putty rather than quick lime, which is very caustic. Goggles, mask and overalls are essential.

Hot white patio

During the long, hot Olhão summer, the patio, or 'quintal', becomes the most used space in the house – an outdoor room to eat, rest during siesta and enjoy the long, balmy nights.

As the sun makes its way over an everlasting sheet of blue sky, it casts interesting shadows – places to read a book out of its glare. In late afternoon the walls seem to come closer, the whites softening to cream, and by sunset they take on a warmish glow.

There's a woman at the market who sells the sweetest figs from her own trees, and bright posies of zinnias to decorate the table

Feasting with white

When there's a crowd to feed, I add extra tables and unify the mismatching surfaces with white cloths. Pure linen is good (see Volga Linen, where they sell extra-large linen cloths ideal for a wedding or larger party), but an inexpensive idea is to use a white cotton sheet.

In the kitchen at home in London, we eat at a work surface-cum-table on wheels (a clever adaptation of Ikea trolley units that an art director used when we had a Jack Dee comedy series shot in the house). I painted the pale wooden frames and shelves in white and, like the white cloth idea, it's a way of unifying the look.

Whitewash, white out, white as snow, pure white, off-white, paper white, bleached white

When dad accidentally tipped over a large tin of white emulsion as he was painting our new house, the terrible expletives and white flood seeping down the steps and drowning the lawn could have put me off the colour before I'd left primary school. The trauma, luckily, was short-lived and it taught me the importance of putting the lid back on the pot of paint.

White notes

White paint is white because it reflects the most light rays away from it. White paint is made from chalk, or zinc, barium or rice. In the past, artists used bone white from burned lambs' bones, shell paints made from seashells, eggshells, oysters and even pearls.

Pure and white, lead paint is the best of white whites, but if absorbed through the skin or ingested as powder, it is deadly. White lead pigment was used by the Romans and Chinese from early on, but people mainly decorated with whites in chalk or lime. European artists used it for hundreds of years as a primer, to mix with pigments to build up colour, and to bring out highlights, such as the shine on a tulip petal in a Dutch still life.

There was nothing to replace lead white in oils until just before the First World War when titanium paint was invented. Later, zinc oxide replaced the noxious qualities of lead. Lead paint is now regulated in decorating and used only for listed buildings. There is no lead in commercial paints, and lead pencils are made with graphite, so chewing on a pencil during double maths won't kill you.

Seaside colours: blue and white Olhão doorway

White houses

White was used for walls and ceilings in the second half of the eighteenth century as a foil for stronger colours. After the excesses of Victorian tastes for sombre, rich colours, the modernist and romantic

Bleached white textures on the terrace

light, white rooms of Charles Rennie Mackintosh and William Morris were a breath of fresh air. In the 1920s and 1930s, titanium oxide created a brighter, more stable white, which was embraced by society decorators such as Syrie Maughan and Elsie de Wolfe, who declared that the way to decorate was with 'plenty of optimism and a lick of white paint'. A girl after my own heart. In the 1990s, design magazines couldn't get enough of the white minimalist look, which seemed to necessitate the removal of any human presence.

White is a contradiction, if you think about it

Hospital whites, say, are as robust and practical as pure white spaces for yoga retreats are ethereal. And white spaces can be as clinical and relentlessly oppressive as they can be calming and relaxing – depending on what you put with them. At the very least, white rooms need to be grounded for everyday life with injections of some texture and colour.

Simple white

White has to be approached with purpose or you lose touch with it. I use it for its simplicity, its space and light-enhancing qualities, and also as a way of drawing together noncontiguous spaces.

And as for finding the perfect shade of white, I look no further than a pot of Dulux brilliant white emulsion. It saves the multiple-choice stress of facing paint charts that confuse with ever-dizzying arrays of whites.

An inventory for the simple white kitchen

I think it's much more interesting to trawl the junk shops and car boot sales for old storage cupboards and sideboards that can be tarted up with a lick of paint than to buy new; pieces that can go with you when you move.

My solution for most of my kitchen storage is a long, open shelf for plates, bowls, glasses and cups. It's good to be able to see what is what. Beneath that is a stainless-steel pole with hooks for daily kit: colander, slotted spoon, cheese grater, potato brush, ladle and all those other essentials.

Apart from the sink and cooker arrangements, I prefer the kitchen to be unfitted

'Have nothing in your house that you do not know to be useful, or believe to be beautiful.'

William Morris

Some kitchen essentials

Pudding basins: the old-fashioned creamy-coloured ones made by Mason Cash.

Blue-and-white enamelware: the more worn and weathered the better.

Le Creuset pans: I buy secondhand ones on eBay.

Candlesticks: I can always find pretty and inexpensive ones from a label called Gisela Graham, or Ikea, of course.

Big white bowls and platters: car boot sales and charity shops are good sources, and I look when the sales are on in department stores like John Lewis.

White jugs: car boot territory, and then specialist vintage markets such as the monthly one at Kempton race course in Surrey.

Simple pottery and stoneware: for natural textures and good for keeping local potters in business (I have a lovely pouring bowl from Jan Pateman, a regular at London's Herne Hill market).

The white table needs little embellishment. I like old-fashioned, creamy-coloured bone-handled knives and simple silver spoons and forks. Again, these are items you can pick up piecemeal from markets and car boot sales; these days it's not necessary to have matching sets. For something more modern and beautifully plain and streamlined, I recommend Robert Welch's 1960s' classic 'RW2 satin' in stainless steel.

Late summer colour with Grace and Constance Spry roses

White and natural kitchen textures at the end of a dusty track in southern Italy

One morning we drive through winding and signpostless back lanes to visit a friend at the Masseria La Furca Nuova. Quite lost, we eventually come upon a very small man packed into a very small van on three wheels who ups the one gear and helpfully leads us to our destination.

Surrounded by weathered stone-blocked walls including an 'agrumito' courtyard with scented orange and lemon trees, it was built about 150 years ago to house the animals, farm equipment and drying areas for tobacco, figs and tomatoes, for the larger Masseria La Furca a couple of kilometres away.

Overlooking a panorama of olive groves and, on the horizon, a blue paint stroke of sea, everything about this farmhouse near Lecce in Salento, Puglia, is finely detailed and beautifully executed by its owner.

Constructed from blocks of 'pietra Leccese' (Lecce sand and limestone), a local material that comes from the nearby quarries of Cursi, the exterior is plastered in natural earth plaster, once light pink but now dark with age.

Inside, the walls and lofty stella-vaulted ceilings are finished with smooth, polished plaster and white limewash. The ceiling in the main entrance room has had the plaster taken off to expose the stone.

The kitchen is a home cook's dream, with functional wood and metal tables, kitchen units made from stone blocks with travertine marble tops, and smooth white floors in 'pietra Leccese' slabs, untreated so that they remain natural and matt. There are local ceramics and rustic green Japanese pots for detail. Reflecting the sense of peace and simplicity throughout the house, the kitchen also seems a favourite place for Paloma, the lovely grey cat.

I never tire of Olhão's white cubist skyline or the whitewashed houses and stairways leading to heavenly terraces for sunning or simply hanging out the washing.

Filipe Monteiro and his partner Eleonor have created a calm, elegant white courtyard retreat at the heart of Convento, a townhouse with rooms to rent, in Olhão. Like entering Dr Who's Tardis, you pass from a narrow alley through an unassuming white door into a world of seductive white detail, from whitewashed walls to soft white furnishings and bedrooms with crisp white sheets.

There are touches of colour in the traditional blue-and-white floor tiles, and the limpid blue pool on the rooftop terrace with its views over the sea.

Continuing my journey in white
I come across Convento, Olhão, a
white retreat with simple detailing

I dream of sleeping in a dry bath of cold, clean linen

Furnishing a bedroom in white is no problem if you have a paintbrush and a pot of white paint to hand. I slap the white onto everything from a four poster from Ikea with a very nasty shiny dark-brown varnish to a junk wardrobe from the local Geranium charity shop for the blind. I am lazy and use emulsion because it is quick drying and has a matt texture, but for a piece that needs to be more resilient, such as a chest of drawers, I use a tougher oil-based eggshell finish.

White and wooden floor textures are natural colour companions

At Convento, in Olhão, honey-coloured wooden floors are a warm and textural contrast with the all-white bedroom interiors.

A stair-runner effect is an inexpensive way to create contrasting colour and texture and is also practical, because it will wear better than if the treads were painted all white.

On a visit to the fleamarket in Fuseta, a Sunday morning wash strung out on the line in the early spring Algarve sunshine gives me an idea for using orange and turquoise-blue detail in the white bathroom.

Splashes of colour on white

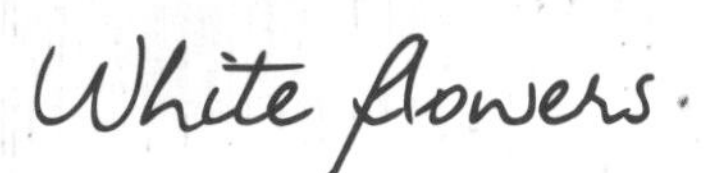

Creamy Wallflowers

Another 'Spring Green'

'Spring Green' Tulip

Rose 'Winchester Cathedral'

White hyacinths at Christmas + in spring

Dying but beautiful parrot tulip

'Iceberg' Roses

I don't repel; I welcome the tendrils of white jasmine that tumble over the fence from my neighbour's garden. I greet this invader with a pair of secateurs to cut sprigs of scented white flowers to put beside the bed.

Lemon ice cream

For a Brazilian caipirinha-style experience, replace the lemons with limes and serve with shots of cachaça.

3 lemons
200g/7oz/1 cup sugar
450ml/¾ pint/2 cups double cream

Finely grate the rind of I lemon. Squeeze the juice of all 3 and combine with the rind and the sugar. Whip the cream and fold into the sugar mixture. Pour into a shallow container (stainless steel freezes quicker than plastic) and freeze for a few hours until solid around the outside and mushy in the middle. Stir with a fork, then freeze until firm.

... and a simple white garden

Artist Mandy Bonnell had a shock when 'basically the whole garden' was taken out by a corrugated iron roof blown off the next-door property during a winter storm. Nestling between the high London walls of her terraced flat in Bermondsey, the garden is Mandy's art and her muse. There was no question that it had to be put back together again. And that is what Mandy did, buying new plants, and starting more from seed.

When I visited in the following May, there were already pink and purple delphiniums and agapanthus about to come into bloom. Gravel paths and low-level box hedging gave it the feel of an Elizabethan knot garden. Mandy bought basic trellis from the DIY store, giving it coats of white paint to create structural detail and to give the sense of entering an intimate outdoor haven.

Saffron, quince and summer beaches

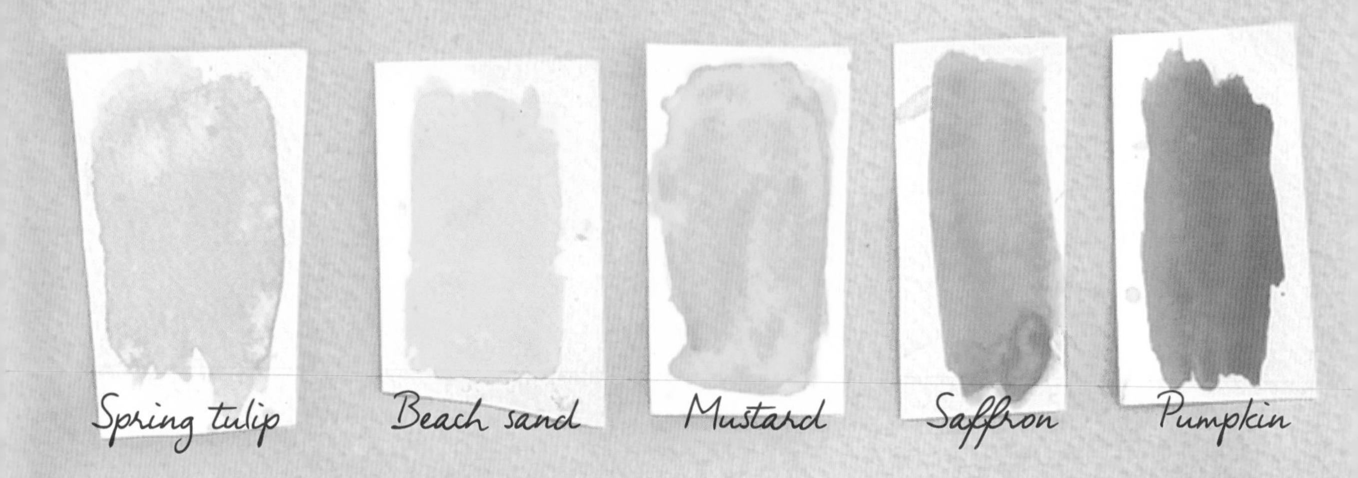

Yellow is such an in-your-face, optimistic colour that you'd expect it to be used in more, rather than fewer, situations. But as the lightest, brightest colour in the spectrum, it needs careful editing. My favourite yellows are mustard shades with a hint of green, like the apples in the garden that turn golden as autumn advances.

Jane Cumberbatch
pure style
making
From white paint and shortbread to pea pods and
baking
how to make life richer and more creative
raking
simple ideas and everyday ingredients
4/6
Summer Cooking contains over a thousand recipes from all over the world - for table, buffet, or picnic. Elizabeth David is well known for the infectious enthusiasm with which she has handled French, Italian, and Mediterranean cookery: she imparts the same quality to this selection of summer dishes that are light (not necessarily cold), easy to prepare, and based on the meat and vegetables in season.
Demonstrating how an unconventional use of herbs can lend interest to the simplest meal, the author describes some forty ways of coping, for example, with the familiar egg, from the Provençal *oeufs pochés* to *Moonshine*, a recipe from the seventeenth century. She is no less resourceful in her chapters on *hors d'oeuvre*, summer soups, fish and meat of various kinds, vegetables, sauces, and sweets.
Summer Cooking succeeds in bringing the cool, fresh flavour of garden, fields, and sea into the kitchen and dining-room.
Cover photograph by Anthony Denney
endive
Violet
FONTE NATURAL DE ÓMEGA-3
TRADIÇÃO AÇORES
BOM
PETISCO
ATUM POSTA EM ÓLEO VEGETAL
grated rind and juice of 2 lemons
2 egg yolks
50 g/2oz/½ stick butter
175g/6oz/generous 3/4 cup sugar

Fresh yellows for ceramics and sunflowers

The Saturday Andalucian market in Aracena is a good place to pick up simple yellow bowls with swirls of bright green glaze. They evoke the Andalucian landscape, bleached yellow in summer and dotted with marching rows of green olive trees.

Then there are sunflowers, whole fields crammed with huge yellow flower heads stretching towards the sun like sunbathers on the first day of the holiday.

Yellow and green detail from the landscape decorates an Olhão front door

Brighter than Prozac

I've talked before about retreating to the cool and shade of my bedroom when it's too damn hot and bright outside to work on the laptop. The room faces north and so it is very useful for this purpose, but conversely it needs a cheer up, especially when summer slides into cooler autumn.

A shot of yellow in the silk mustard-yellow dress hanging on the cupboard, is the kind of light colour touch to lift the mood.

A hint of bright pink to make yellow sing

Yellowcake is the colour: cool, bright and so intense that the eye is lost in its yellowness. After two coats I want to put my sunglasses on. Its strength highlights what I wrote about at the beginning of the book, that to get the full value of a unique colour, it must have other hues by its side. Artist Winifred Nicholson described a bunch of yellow flowers that didn't say 'yellow' until she added two everlasting sweet peas in magenta pink, when all her yellows broke into luminosity.

When I take her advice and add white furniture, tableware and yellow's complementary colours in shots of violet and pink detail, Yellowcake becomes a colour to seriously consider.

Walking in Brockwell Park, we skirt round roped-off tree trunks where a swarm of bees has set up home. Then, lying on the grass and looking up at the sky, imagine that the country is in town. I pick up a fallen pink moss rose and take it home and set it on a piece of yellow fabric by my desk like visual elevenses.

I imagine using the sun-dried grass yellows and limpid sea blues of Italy's Puglia in a fabric and paint combination at home

SHIPS
15 WARNE
SEASHELLS
70 WARNE
TREES
HORSES & PONIES
9 WARNE
WILD ANIMALS
ANCIENT & ROMAN BRITAIN
CACTI
SEA & SEASHORE

The handpainted border detail strikes a note with me because the Pure Style borders are based on the idea of simple embellishment and the Swedish travelling players from Drottningholm who took decorative paper panels with them as a little bit of home.

Everyday browns and yellows for tiles at the entrance to an Olhão corner shop; and a cottage at Skansen Open Air Museum in Stockholm.

Sand and honey colours in Italian baroque beauty and English autumn leaves

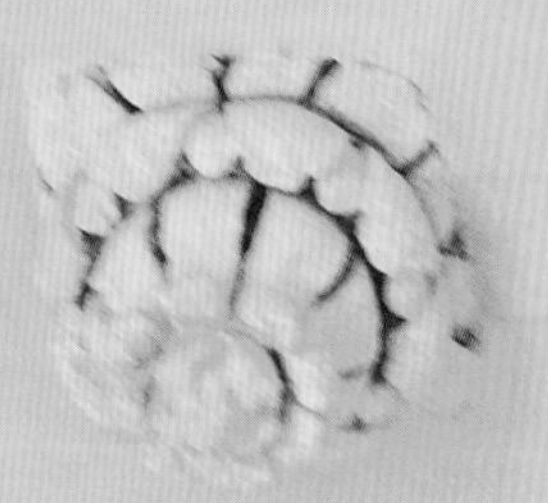

I am footsore and thirsty in the late-afternoon heat after drinking in the colour and textural beauty of dazzling seventeenth-century white limestone baroque churches, palaces and Roman remains in Lecce, Puglia. It's like being in Florence and Seville both at the same time and finding gems in every nook, corner, alleyway and piazza. See this vaulted ochre ceiling in the Government Palace, a former convent.

Yellow ochre on the street
in Stockholm

Yellow and blue blanket advice

Every home should have at least one yellow and one blue checked blanket, if only to be able to throw them on a plain-coloured chair for sunny decoration, but more importantly to cocoon around oneself while reading a good book in front of the fire.

Dayroom Yellow is a warm, buttery colour, very good for making a small, dark attic room feel sunny.

When we lived in the Spitalfields area of London, I painted the sitting room in a similar shade and added a worn kilim, pale terracotta checks and wood textures to give it a timeless country feel. The room felt welcoming at any time of day, and at night pools of light, rather than anything overhead, intensified the yellowness and made it feel wonderfully cosy.

Yellow notes

Brilliant yellow nasturtiums

It is golden September, warm for the time of year I hear, but under clouds like grey wadding, the garden looks bleak, dull green and downcast. Except for a little oasis of brilliance by the fence on the right where a patch of self-seeded nasturtiums shine in the midday gloom; an almost defiant mass of trumpet-shaped flowers of iridescent yellows streaked with orange. They seem unnatural, as if the flowers are artificially lit in some way or other. Going back to colour physics, this is explained by the fact that yellow is the colour nearest to white light, and why pure yellows exude light and brightness. Van Gogh wrote: 'Now we are having beautiful warm, windless weather that is very beneficial to me. The sun, a light that for lack of a better word I can only call yellow, bright sulphur yellow, pale lemon gold. How beautiful yellow is!'

Any colour that's so exuberantly cheerful must have a darker underbelly, and with yellow it is the sallow, sickly yellows of decay, poison and general malaise. In Charlotte Perkins Gilman's feminist classic about a woman ordered to a yellow bedroom to rest and pull herself together, she finds that the tortuous pattern of the wallpaper winds its way into to the recesses of her mind. 'It is the strangest yellow, that wallpaper! It makes me think of all the yellow things I ever saw – not beautiful ones like buttercups, but old, foul, bad yellow things ... It creeps all over the house.'

Remnant of Swedish yellow check woven cotton

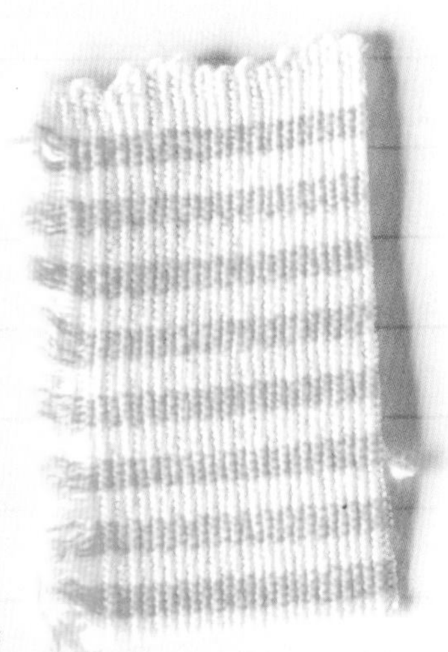

Living with yellow

Yellow stands next to orange and green on a colour wheel. Depending on the amount of blue or red tints it contains, yellow has different qualities.

Cool yellows

Yellows with hints of blue are cool, clear and luminous, like the delicate flowers on rocket when it has gone to seed. Clear lemon yellow, for example, was popular in the late nineteenth century when it was contrasted with amethyst green. Bright yellows are far too distracting and irritating to go to bed with or to pen a novel by in the office, but very good for a sunny look in kitchens and dining rooms.

For reference, visit the fresh yellow drawing room restored to its 1830s' brilliance at Sir John Soane's house in London's Lincoln's Inn. At Monet's house at Giverney, there's the famous yellow dining room – and blue kitchen – painted in two tones of cool yellow, offset by bright blues in fabric and china. In my styling days on House & Garden we had great fun with a 'Monet dining room' shoot, sourcing Provençal prints, ceramics and the yellowest yellow paint, which I discovered at John Oliver, a brilliant paint specialist, sadly no longer in business.

Yellow Brixton balcony

Closer to home, on the way past my dog-walking route through Brockwell Park, there's a year-long beam of cheerfulness from a third-floor corner balcony in a bland inter-war housing block decorated with bright yellow walls and window boxes with greenery and pink blooms in summer.

PS Pale- and blue-grey work well with cool yellows. Mauves are the complement of cool yellows and hints of these in a room can bring the colour alive.

Warm yellows

Yellows with red tones (in nasturtiums and the richer sunflowers) are warm and welcoming. They have gentle, more golden hues, which are especially good in north-facing rooms, and look sunny even on a dark day. Warm ochre-coloured yellows go well with lead grey, light brown, celadon green, lavender or grey-blue. A warm yellow is a great idea for adding depth to a small room in a rental space. You can see dull, warm ochre yellows made from natural pigments on historic buildings from Seville to Stockholm, and any number of village houses across Europe. Ochres were the yellows of the house painter's paintbox and give mellow warmth to any interior. If dull yellow is used with cold greys and blues, its yellowness is accentuated, whereas alongside warm, earthy colours it appears more neutral.

Finding yellow in the market

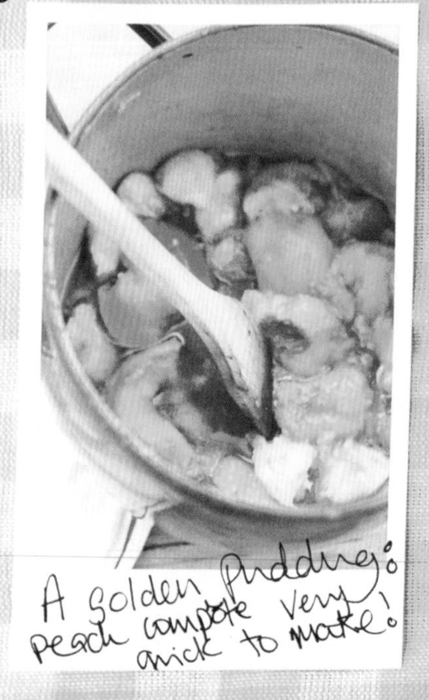

Plan a yellow feast with a tray of roasted tomatoes, pumpkins and squashes or golden fruit salad with peaches and melons.

A recipe for peach compote: Good for using overripe peaches. Blanch in boiling water for a few minutes, then remove the skins. Slice the flesh, add to a saucepan with water to just cover, add 2–3 tablespoons brown sugar and a squeeze of lemon. Simmer for 15 minutes or until soft. Cool, then eat with crème fraîche.

Add a handful of peppery flavoured nasturtium leaves and flowers to a green salad

Purple, mustards and greys from the hedgerows

St Jude's fabrics, run by Simon and Angie Lewin, collaborate with artists to create fabrics and prints that have a retro twentieth-century feel, with patterns that make you think of country lanes winding below tall hedgerows and with cottages tucked in secret vales. An autumn meadow has landed with this grassy printed linen in mustard and grey. It looks great against painted grey-green walls, while the purple cotton makes a good foil in cushions.

Swatch box yellows

MissPrint, Little Trees in Yellow,
linen/cotton/nylon mix
Bluebellgray,
Teal Butterfly, linen
Les Indiennes, Papillon in
Gold, cotton
The Art of Wallpaper, Bernard Thorp, Ivy Wallpaper
The Art of Wallpaper, Bernard
Thorp, 3-inch stripe wallpaper
Zimmer + Rohde, Score, 112 polyester, velour

Rhubarb and custard colours

These are rich shades to put together on a rooftop terrace or seaside verandah somewhere very hot and exotic like a Caribbean plantation house or a Rio beach retreat. However, if these lie beyond pocket or possibility, settle for the look *chez vous*: make a simple tie-on bedhead in yellow and contrast it with pillowcases in pink – both are easy to run up on the sewing machine.

Mellow yellows

I bought this pair of chairs from the local secondhand shop on Streatham Hill, and updated them with blue and mustard-coloured linen throws to hide the past-their-prime covers.

Yellow Babouschka door and grey walls: one of my favourite colour duos

Golden yellow with hot pinks and oranges

The interior decorator David Hicks designed some brilliant pink and orange combinations in fabrics and wallpapers back in the 1960s, when colour was new, exciting and very unBritish.

Hanging on the peg, a Diane von Fürstenburg wrap dress in pink and orange geometrics is a piece of interior decoration in itself.

I like the way the sartorial Sevillano looks dashing in hot pink swim shorts or vividly patterned shirt, like a strutting beach peacock, and with more than a nod to the matador bullfight tradition

RDE DEL CAMINO
FERIA
14 al 18
Agosto
2013
ALÍA DE CULTURA Y FESTEJOS
O DE VALVERDE DEL CAMINO

I'm going on a crab apple hunt with dog, pair of steps and a green mesh collecting bag. We're based under a laden tree which spills over the pavement at Malcolm's house, a fellow location owner. Help yourself. So I am. The tree is dropping its fruit fast, and dozens of pink and yellow crabs decorate the pavement.

Crab apple jelly

Makes 4–6 x 250g/8oz jars

2kg/4lb 8oz crab apples
about 500g/1lb 2oz/
2½ cups granulated sugar

Wash and chop the crab apples and put them in a pan with just enough water to cover. Bring to the boil, then simmer until soft. Stir occasionally and mash the apples once or twice with a potato masher to really break them up and extract the pectin.

Ladle the fruit and juice into a bag made from muslin (place a large square of muslin across a bowl, lay the fruit in the middle and gather up the sides with string). I hang this bag from a hook on the rail above my sink and allow the juice to drip into the bowl overnight. Don't squeeze the bag or the jelly will be cloudy.

Pour the strained juice back into the pan and add the sugar. As a guide, use 500g/1lb 2oz/ 2½ cups sugar per 500ml/17fl oz/ 2 cups of extracted juice. Stir over a low heat to dissolve the sugar, then bring to the boil.

Boil rapidly, stirring all the time, until setting point is reached. This takes about 20 minutes. The jelly is set if a teaspoonful wrinkles when pushed with a spoon on an ice-cold plate. When ready, pot in jars that have been washed thoroughly and sterilized in a hot oven for a few minutes.

Lipstick and pink petals

Reds and pinks are powerful colours. Primary-school red poster paints are a little too obvious, and sugary princess pinks don't do modern femininity any favours, but there's something so uplifting about a powdery Suffolk pink cottage, or a jug of bright fuchsia or shocking-pink roses.

I was reminded of the power of pink when reading my book on the tube a few months ago when I noticed a handsome guy looking intently at me. I was flattered by the attention until he leaned over and asked, 'Where did you get that pink lipstick?' It was not the first time that my pink lipstick had been seen before the person wearing it ... or maybe it was a chat-up line, after all.

happy 2013
MARISCOS
Isidoro
Rhubarb from 'The Yorkshire Triangle' - to be roasted with sugar + orange zest

Splashes of red in a shady patio

Antonia Williams is a painter whose time is split 50:50 between Olhão and London. Her patio is cool and shady and feels almost Central American with its lush greenery and bright-red detailing. She chose the colour oil-based Barbot Acetinado 2024 because, as she explains: 'It is a very clear, particular colour, somewhere between hot pink and tomato, somehow reminiscent of a fifties' Max Factor lipstick. I love it, as being very interested in what makes a colour so special, it constantly reminds me of how a subtle change to an ordinary pillar-box red can make all the difference in the world. It is best when freshly put on, as the bright sun here in Portugal bleaches it slightly, but it still holds its own for a year or two. I probably wouldn't have been brave enough without the enthusiasm of a friend, but the red seems to complement the yellows in the courtyard, and contrasts well with the huge tropical plants.'

In my Olhão patio, a few streets from Antonia, the grey tones of a painted back door and the whitewashed wall are offset by a splash of red-striped linen at the cold-only outside shower (fabulous in summer; punishing otherwise). I picked up the traditional Portuguese washstand dumped on a local street and literally carried it home on my shoulder. I checked with the woman who was looking at me quizzically from the next door window, but she shrugged in the affirmative.

Italian reds

Walking along the olive groves and dusty tracks of the Puglian countryside, I spy the red limewashed walls of an old farmhouse. Peeling and fading, it is at one with the gnarled olive trees, baked red earth and dried grasses.

Not far away in another grove of shady olives, I come upon another timeless red colour decorating a higgledy-piggle of laminated 1970s' kitchen units in a farmer's outdoor kitchen.

I love the unintended, stylish and upcycled look

Painter Piers de Laszlo has decorated the corridor in his house with the blue room in grey and scarlet detail to create an Olhão baroque effect

The same red pigment, mixed with limewash, adds vibrancy to the narrow galley kitchen and is contrasted with simple green wood pot hooks and traditional Portuguese tiles.

Cochineal and cool greens

I ease open the lid on the tin of carmine-coloured Cochineal emulsion and wonder, frankly, how overpowering it will look. But I am knocked out by its rich and lustrous tones. It fills this north-facing room with luminosity. Contrasting details in cool green glass dishes, pale green-blue furniture, and stick of green rhubarb decoration keep the strong colour in its place.

With red a symbol of passion and blood, the painted orange-red gates to the Plaza de Toros in Valverde del Camino, Andalucia (where to buy the best riding boots in Spain) couldn't be more fitting

Warm and brilliant reds

Carmine-coloured peonies (the parents of which I relocated to my own garden when my mother died) show to what brilliant extremes the colour red can go compared with the more muted reds in a Stockholm junk shop's street display. The faded terracotta kilim and peeling warm red-painted bucket are starting points for a simple, natural look with greys or sludgy greens as background colour.

I've just come back from the last day of the Winifred Nicholson exhibition at the Dulwich Picture Gallery in London, where a warm red is a rich canvas for the permanent display of paintings in the main gallery.

Tap the taut green skin, and if it sounds hollow, the fruit is ripe. Chill the watermelon in the fridge, then slice it into cool, sweet-juiced, fleshy, orange-pink chunks on a hot summer afternoon. Buy local – it doesn't travel. PS See Frida Kahlo's watermelons for inspiration.

The produce at the outdoor market in Cisternino, Puglia is a visual and edible jewel compared to supermarket-land with its piles of three for one obesity-guaranteed snacks and biscuits

Tomato summer reds

I am dazzled by the glossy piles of melons, crates of green rocket and plump white mozzarella sloshing around in baths of milk. Summer is defined by the stalls weighed down with box upon box of orange-red and pink tomatoes. Ripened in baked earth under a blazing sun, they taste so sweet, nothing like the bland and anaemic ones compromised by life in a polytunnel. Later, we make a salad from our tomato treasures: sliced, seasoned with sea salt, sprigs of basil and olive oil – pure luxury.

Manuel Canovas,
Balata in Piment,
cotton
Sheila Coombes,
Simply Stonewash,
in Lavender, linen
Pure Style border, Rose Petal
Osborne & Little,
Lorca,
Montcalm, cotton
Manuel Canovas,
Belinda in Rose,
lambswool
Romo, Linara
in Begonia,
cotton/linen
MissPrint, Saplings in Cream/Pink wallpaper
Liberty, Rosa,
B, tana lawn
Sheila Coombes,
Simply Stonewash
in Plaster, linen
Osborne & Little, Lorca,
Louisiane, cotton
Osborne & Little,
Lorca, La Favorite,
cotton

Swatch box reds

The Art of Wallpaper, Belynda Sharples, Daisy

Manuel Canovas, Edouard in Rose Indien, cotton/viscose

Checks, stripes, soft cottons and not a hint of Barbie pink

Manuel Canovas, Balleroy in Azalee, cotton

Pierre Frey, Grenadines in Multi Colore, linen/polyester

Bluebellgray, Fumiko, linen

Red and pink notes

Rose-pink geranium petal

Pure red is neither yellowish nor bluish. Red is the badge of revolution and physical passions. Reds can go from demonic and halloweenish red-orange on black to cupcake-icing pale pink.

Scarlet and lipstick pinks

The brightest red is scarlet, without a trace of blue. Back in the day, scarlets were derived from kermes, tiny grain-like insects which fed on berries of Middle Eastern oak trees. Hence the origin of the expression 'dyed in the grain'.

When the conquistadors invaded South America in the 1500s, they exported dried cochineal, carmine-coloured pigment extracted from the crushed carcasses of the female *Dactylopius coccus*, a cactus-feeding scale insect used by the Aztecs for dyeing their vibrant-coloured fabrics.

By 1645, Cromwell's New Model Army wore red coats, and the scarlet broadcloth for British officers' uniforms was dyed with cochineal until as late as 1952. Today, cochineal is harvested mainly in Peru and the Canary Islands on plantations of prickly pear. About 70,000 insects are needed to produce half a kilo of dye.

Otherwise known as colour additive E120, cochineal is not a vegetarian's friend as it used in everything from a Starbuck's Strawberry Frappuchino to the pink smudge on my wine glass from my favourite shocking-pink lipstick. Around the age of nine, when my mother trusted me with using the gas cooker, I enjoyed solo Saturday afternoon bake-offs. Peppermint essence was exciting enough to flavour mint creams, but adding drops of beetroot-purple cochineal colouring to turn yellow butter icing pink was like being a medieval alchemist.

Tomato reds work with greens and whites

When thinking about decorating with reds, the complementary of crimsons and carmines is a yellow-green. Splashes of crimson also go well with violet, yellow and orange. Deep red, the colour of rich, red apples, is bluer, and with complementary olive green is also good for dining rooms. When lit by candlelight, it seems to glow with extra warmth.

Pinks and purples from my daughter's Indian travels

Blue-reds also include rich fuchsia pink, a colour that works as a vibrant splash against backgrounds of green or blue or yellow. Fuchsia pinks come into their own in southern climates where their colour is intensified by brighter light. But there is a case for bringing such flamboyant shades into northern spaces, such as a jug of pink tulips on a dull English day in January. Shocking pink was 1930s' Italian fashion designer and surrealist artist, Elsa Schiaparelli's signature colour. She described hot pink as 'bright, impossible, impudent, becoming life-giving, like all the light and the birds and the fish in the world put together, a colour of China and Peru but not of the West'.

The colour purple

The colour purple or violet is the bluest end of red. Although it became the colour of Roman emperors, purple dye was extracted from the humble murex sea snail. After the battle of Pompey, Caesar gave himself the sole privilege of wearing a full-length toga in this mollusc-dyed purple.

The Japanese made purple dye from the borage family 'murasaki-so', known in English as gromwell. It decorated the costume and tassels of the highest ranking sumo referee.

When William Perkin created the first analine dye stuff in London in 1856, his particular mauve colour became known as magenta, after the battle of Magenta in 1859. Fashion-conscious women in crinolines, and later bustles, invested in mauve for a decade or so.

My own experience of purple is not the happiest, as it was the colour of my school uniform: purple blazer, purple sweater, purple scratchy culottes for games and a humiliating purple beret.

However, purple and green are fabulous colour combinations in the garden, as you can see in the chapter on green. Purple is a hard colour to live with en masse, but paler tones of lilacs and violet are pleasing and go with green detail very well.

What is pink?

Pink is generally defined as a colour intermediate between red and white. There are so many different tones ranging from pale salmon pink to rich and vibrant shocking fuchsia pink.

The most nauseous candy-floss pinks dominate the female baby and pre-teen market, as well as anything that belongs to the world of cupcake icing.

I see the prettiest raspberry pinks on traditional houses all over the Algarve, and then in eastern England there is famous Suffolk pink, used to decorate cottages and medieval moated halls. In the past, the shades were created by adding elderberries, dried blood or crumbled red earth to limewash.

This rich pink is called Nancy's Blushes, and whoever Nancy may be, or whether this really reflects her cheek colour, it is a fresh and vibrant colour for decorating with and not in the least cloying. I like to contrast a paler but rich pink like this with cooler blue-green detail. This shade will also look great with shots of pink, mustard, brown and white.

A lick of pink

Like ringing the changes with a necklace or shoelaces for trainers, a pink-striped paper border is a simple tool for adding colour and interest to a white wall.

This is a very good idea for renters who want inexpensive and temporary decoration. And it's an even more attractive proposition with house prices being so out of reach for first-time buyers.

Rose-petal pinks

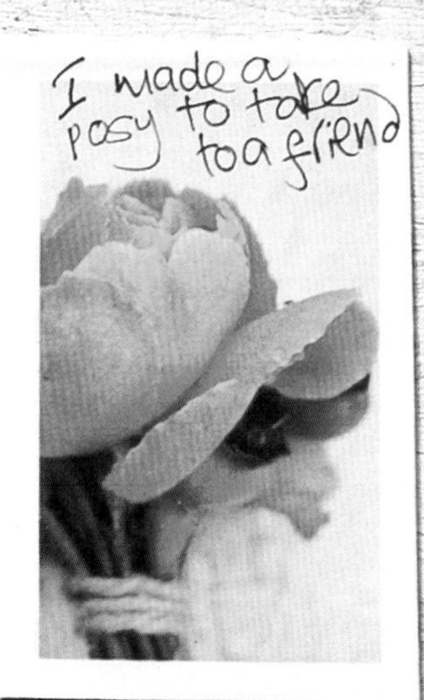

For a few weeks in June I display a home-grown version of the Chelsea Flower Show in Tulse Hill, when the garden, as my grandma would say, 'looks a picture' of blousy rose blooms. The flowers continue with diminishing but still beautiful effect through the summer, and then even into December, when I cut the last frosted buds and powder-puff petals of the year.

More pink updates

Extend the possibilities of a pink border and use it around a door frame

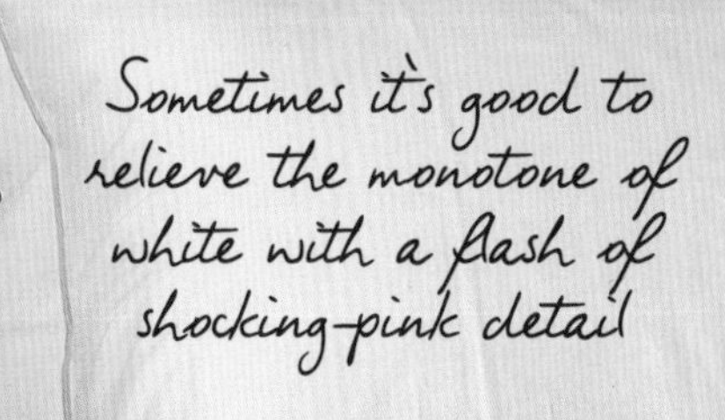

Sometimes it's good to relieve the monotone of white with a flash of shocking-pink detail

Patio lights in upcycled fishing traps from Sagres in Portugal

Gorgeous pink cushions in fabric from the Cloth Shop in London's Soho are all that's needed to bring an exuberant splash of colour to this whitewashed courtyard. This is part of the restoration project by architect Filipe Monteiro at Casa da Luz – originally built in 1786 – and one of the oldest houses in Olhão.

The baroque-arched living and dining areas were used as a metal workshop for many years, and from the 1940s as Olhão's scout hut.

The patio tables and benches are designed by Mestre João Pedro of Belo Romão, in three-crown Portuguese Pinus pinaster timber from the Ribatejo.

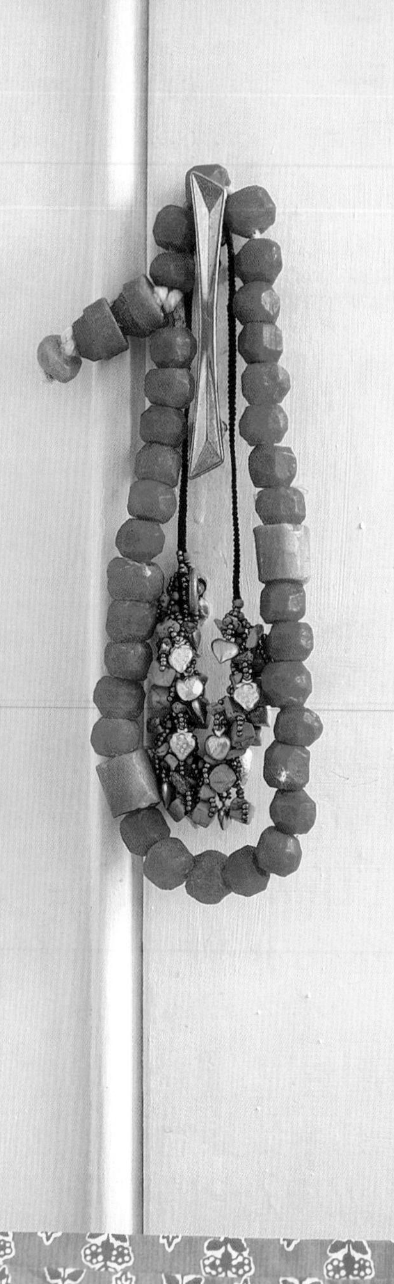

Modern pinks

My youngest daughter returned from an adventure in colour on her recent trip to India. Of Jaipur she writes: 'Roamed the bustling streets and bought pigments and glasses that they use at the chai stalls. It's the one that is known as the Pink City, but it's more orange.' Inspired, I fished out the pink handblocked printed cotton chair covers made up years ago from a length of vintage Laura Ashley.

Shocking-pink cotton velvet from Manuel Canovas would be the perfect extravagance for warmth and colour all winter; and also gives a fresh look to country garden Colefax and Fowler wallpaper florals

A raspberry ripple of tulips

Very frilly 'matchpoint'

'Flig Flag'

'spring green' white tulip with pinks etc.

The 'Triumph' tulips remind me of rasbery ripple icecream

'Lilac Perfectin'

I buy most of my tulip bulbs online, and over-order, as there will always be a few failures. The key thing is to plant the bulbs the right way up: hairy bit at the bottom and the pointy shoot at the top.

Jeffrey, our Dutch lodger's, birthday cake

Tulip petals are edible!

Jeffrey's cake

250g/9oz/2¼ sticks unsalted butter, plus extra for greasing
250g/9oz/1¼ cups caster sugar
5 large eggs, beaten
250g/9oz/2 cups self-raising flour

Preheat the oven to 180°C/350°F/gas 4 and grease two 20cm/8in cake tins.

Cream the butter and sugar together until pale and fluffy. Beat in the eggs, then fold in the flour using a metal spoon.

Pour the mixture into the tins and bake in middle of the preheated oven for about 40 minutes until golden and springy to the touch.

Turn out the sponges on to a wire rack and leave to cool while you make the butter icing.

110g/3¾ oz/1 stick unsalted butter, softened
175g/6oz/1¾ cups icing sugar, sifted
160g/5½oz good-quality dark chocolate
2 tbsp milk

Cream the butter and icing sugar together until soft. Melt the chocolate in a bowl over a pan of gently simmering water.

Beat the milk into the buttercream, then add the melted chocolate and beat until light, smooth and shiny.

Use half the icing to sandwich the cakes together, then cover the cakes with the remaining icing and mark a pattern in the top using the tines of a fork.

Blackcurrant ice cream

See the lemon ice cream recipe on page 136 and replace the lemon juice and rind with 200g/7oz topped-and-tailed blackcurrants gently simmered for 5 minutes in 2 tablespoons water and 2 tablespoons sugar.

Linen, hemp and cloud colours

What I mean by natural colours is all the softer browns, greys, blues and greens of sun-bleached driftwood, pebbles and shells – colours that are more peaceful and understated. For inspiration, I also look to the cool, moody interiors and distinctive grey-themed palate of the Danish painter Vilhelm Hammershøi (1864–1916).

two rooms into one, even
before the contracts hav
ritual of the type practised by
tom cats.
Style Insider Jane Cumberpatch
Author of the most stylish style book to come out recently (and we have fashion god Calvin Klein's word on Pure Style), Jane Cumberpatch is clearly someone whose word we can take on what is and is not stylish.
So prepare to make a lot of Spotted Dick, because Jane has chosen her pudding basin as her favourite thing. "It's just basic and functional, cream stoneware," she says. "You can get it in any hardware store."And it's been around forever, she points out. Most people can remember licking mum's cake mixture out of one of these. "A nice simple, solid-shape," which is just the way Jane likes it.
These pudding basins have a thickened rim, and come in different sizes. "The little ones I use to plant hyacinths in. The bigger ones I fill and put on the table — they look quite smart."
And, most importantly, they don't break, "which is useful when there are children around".
T G Green's puddings bowls are available in John Lewis, et al, at £3.75 for a wee one, to £4.95 for a chunky one.
47
Grilled sardines
- shiny, steely shapes

Grey in a hot climate

Eight years ago when I found the house in Olhão, it was in a poor state with damp walls covered in mould and peeling limewash. In the courtyard was a well with evil-smelling contents and a cloud of resident mosquitos.

None of this deterred me, or detracted from the building's tall, elegant proportions and fine woodwork for traditional shutters and double doors that opened on to each of the rooms.

What colour was I to paint the new project? My natural inclination was to go completely down the white route, as a way of opening up and giving cohesion to the space. But then, looking around the local 'ruas', I noticed that grey detail on windows and doors was quite the Olhão thing and thought it a good idea to use it in our house as a way of highlighting the wood detail.

Luis, the painter, made the exterior colour using black pigment in white limewash and carefully painted a grey border around each window frame at the front of the house. For the exterior doors and interior woodwork, I chose an oil-based eggshell in soft blue-grey from a Portuguese paint chart and had it mixed in a local paint shop.

The colours of snails and pantiles

During work on the house in Olhão, we were able to salvage clay pantiles from the roof of the small storehouse in the courtyard. A few were damaged but replacements were found by the builder from his stash of reclaimed building materials. I am so glad that I didn't go for new, plastic, moulded roof tiles; they are very harsh-looking and unnatural.

Spring and summer is the season for snails in the Algarve. 'Hay caracois' at a bar means you can sit with a beer and attend to little dishes of snails, steamed and seasoned with bay, thyme, garlic, onion and piri piri. I have ventured into snail cooking – once.

I came back from a phone call to find the as yet uncooked snails breaking for freedom up and over the pan. I rounded them up and cooked them in the usual way. I thought the results were quite bitter so after that I've left them to the professionals.

Bristle brooms and woven-basket textures

The natural earth colours of woven baskets, chairs, brooms and other household things are as simple and beautiful as they are useful. When we lived in Andalucia, Camilo, a friend in the village, wove us baskets from olive wood. An everyday skill for country people like Camilo, from the generation who had survived famine and poverty during the Spanish Civil War, it was like throwing a cake together for tea. To us it was like receiving a work of art and handmade beauty.

The baskets are with me now, slightly off-centre, which makes them all the more individual. One sits beside the stove for firewood, and the others are great for storing fruit and vegetables.

Natural kitchen

Worn wooden spoons for stirring and tasting are among my favourite kitchen tools, together with chunky terracotta cooking pots. I buy the pots very cheaply in the market and use them to serve up dishes of clams and fish soups. They have the advantage of being both oven and flameproof.

Pierre Frey, Beauregard
Carmin 1, cotton
Sanderson, New Tiger Stripe in Linen/Calico, wallpaper
Pure Style border, Toast
Sheila Coombes, Simply Stonewash in
Nature, cotton
Sheila Coombes, Simply Stonewash
in Shadow, linen
Liberty, Field
of Xanthe
Sunbeams in
Dove, Cotton
Colefax and Fowler, Rothesay Old Blue, linen/polyester mix

Swatch box naturals

Simple black tableware for a table laid with good bread and homemade jam

Spring nettle soup, blazing fires, chairs to fall back and doze in, and gorgeous beds make Ett Hem in Stockholm a luxurious home from home. I am hooked after spending the weekend in this intimate twelve-bedroom hotel designed by Ilse Crawford. I especially like the rustic black tableware by Stockholm potter Birgitta Watz, whose chunky, uneven forms have an almost medieval quality to them, but yet feel very modern.

Fresh green details and earth-coloured natural textures make very good partners

There are no problems in finding beautiful terracotta tiles for house renovation in Olhão and this part of the Algarve. Santa Catarina clay tiles are made from red earth and are stacked by hand when dry, then fired in ancient ovens. They feel smooth to walk on in bare feet and retain the heat of the day in summer for an even more sensual underfoot experience.

Warm terracotta for a sensual barefoot experience

The garden is my comfort zone and all that's in it, from the scent of roses, a blackbird tugging at a worm and the colour of grass in spring, to weathered flower pots, wigwams of hazel sticks and worn, familiar metal watering cans.

3Back to nature

40 pages

Eco garden-

organic

simple plants

simple things to

eat

saving water,

Home

grown

Sand and grey tones go north and south

Honey-coloured and grey Swedish painted detail in an eighteenth-century garden house at Skansen Open Air Museum and woven natural rugs by Swedish company Kasthall.

Grey painted detail and natural woven bits and pieces in the hallway of my house in Olhão

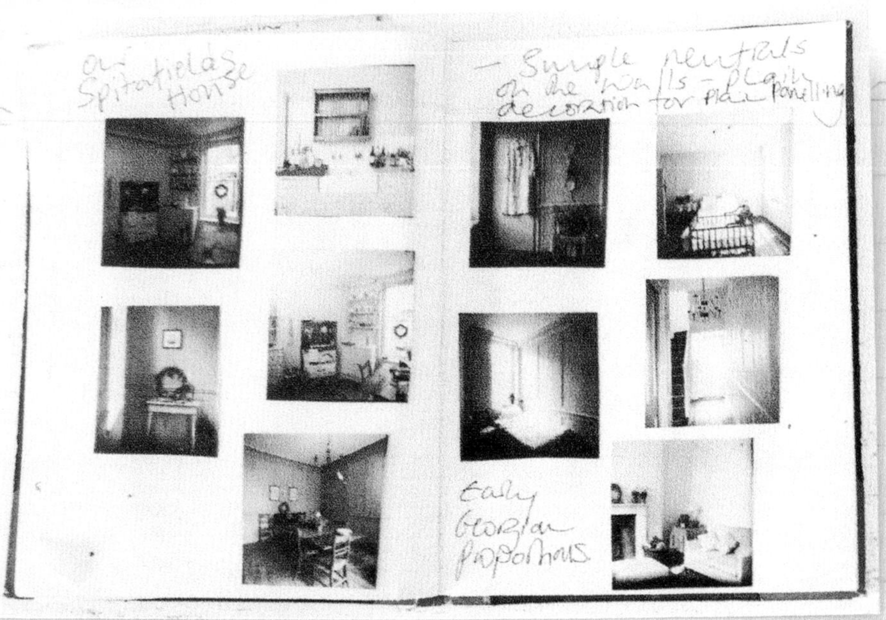

Georgian colours in Spitalfields

If your home belongs to a particular style or period, you can take a cue from the palette of the period. It's not necessary to take historical authenticity too literally, but refer to the tones used and perhaps blend them with colours that make them work today. Keep your choices in tune with the surroundings. In-your-face, strong, synthetic colours are hard enough to live with somewhere urban and modern (I'm not the first one to suggest that some architects are colour blind) but would scream in a rough-hewn stone country cottage. In the 1980s I took on the restoration of a 1726 Georgian terraced house in Spitalfields, a run-down area of East London. A stone's throw from the riches of City banks and bankers, but down-at-heel now for over a century, the area had originally been developed by speculative developers of the day for Huguenot silk merchants.

The worn York stone pavements echoed with history: traces of the Jewish influence lived on in addictive smoked salmon and cream cheese bagels from the 24-hour bagel bakery in Brick Lane. Solly, the fur merchant across the road, had musty wardrobes of mink coats and offered me a made-to-measure fur bikini. The classical Huguenot church at the end of our road had become a synagogue and then morphed more recently, with the influx of the Bangladeshi community, into a mosque. On Friday lunchtime, the vast

doorway would be open, revealing tiers of wooden racks jammed with worshippers' footwear.

The fruit and vegetable market spread beneath the soaring spire of Christchurch. In summer, when the windows were open, I would wake around midnight to the roar of lorries delivering consignments of artichokes from Brittany, the aromatic scents of fresh coriander crushed under tyres, and the flickering glow from bonfires of wooden pallets, warming homeless clients from the soup kitchen in the crypt.

This was my first adventure into playing with colour on any scale.

Our house had been a jeans sweatshop and looked it: fabric remnants, false ceilings, battered floors, walls covered with cheap pine insulation and yellowed with cigarette stains. Was there a house underneath all this neglect?

Over three years, we painstakingly pulled the rotting structure apart and put it back together again. Along the way we uncovered the beautiful wooden panelling designed to enhance the proportions of the rooms, which gave the walls a sense of order and interest. We restored the wooden floors and polished them to maximize reflected light, as the rooms were in shadow from the narrow streets outside.

Fellow restorers in the area were keen on using traditional Georgian colours, but they seemed too strong, too intense, too serious for my taste. I wanted to bring a sense of light and cohesion to the house – to bring it into the twentieth century without losing its integrity. This was long before Farrow & Ball had appeared on the paint scene with its fifty shades of white, and unless one had time to do the mixing, it wasn't easy to find good colours.

My salvation came in the form of a Dulux trade colour card with sludgy off-whites, timeless colours with names like Muffin and Hopsack that perfectly suited my needs. I used eggshell textures, which had a pleasing matt effect. Gloss is banned in my paintbox. First, though, there were months of stripping off the old paint with a blowtorch. It was worth it. I think we put the soul back into the house and it was a huge wrench when we moved out eleven years, three children and one hamster later.

At the house in Spitalfields, we painted the simple wood panelling in understated country cream, olive and stone colours

A found bird's nest; a box of my sister's hen's eggs; a handblocked cotton heart print and weathered painted metal furniture all give me inspiration

Natural defences

Twigs woven onto a metal frame camouflage a storage room at Rosendal, a haven of flowers with orchards of blossoming apple trees and the largest commercial organic garden in Stockholm. Similarly, sheets of split cane create simple and natural window decoration, and allow privacy, in a neighbouring house in Olhão.

Note the grey limewashed decoration that I have also used at home

Nature table

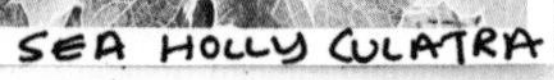

When I was ten, I curated a suburban branch of the Natural History Museum on the shelf of the white bookcase in my bedroom.

There were fossils, shells, driftwood and even a small bird's nest. I continue to come back from the beach or a walk in woods with a leaf, or seed pod, or coloured stone that has sought me out with its shape, beauty and colour.

Lavender-coloured greys for café tables in Stockholm

Because of their very neutrality, naturals are at home in both northern and southern latitudes

Shades of grey: cushions on painted cement seating on a terrace in Puglia, Italy

An attic eyrie in a grey-green, the colour of galvanized metal watering cans

Mr and Mrs Campbell were young marrieds when they moved from Electric Avenue in Brixton to their brand new house in Tulse Hill. When we moved here, eleven years ago, over a century later, remnants of the household lingered like material ghosts. Battered cane sticks nestling in hooks above the windows in the shed where Mrs Campbell took afternoon tea were once hung with linen. Mr Campbell's attic man-cave remained lined with wood panelling and housed a hefty wooden work bench, hooks in the ceiling for gym rings and a skipping rope discarded in a corner of a dusty cupboard.

I chose a colour like that of the Campbell's old grey galvanized watering cans. It's called Pigeon, which is all right if referring to one of the soft grey wood pigeons that land in groups of four pairs in the garden on an outing from their home in Brockwell Park, but not so inspiring if it refers to the average tatty engine-oil-coloured London variety.

I chose a matt emulsion throughout rather than painting the wood in oil-based eggshell, which is what one is supposed to do for woodwork. This leaves the option for the space to be given a less arduous and time-consuming make-over (emulsion dries quicker than oil-based paints) by one of the photo shoots that often use the house. (The deal is that the room is always painted back to this colour again.)

It's worth the climb up flights of stairs to the wood-lined bedroom and bathroom, tucked away at the top of the house

The colour changes with the light in really pleasing ways: in the afternoon when the sun pours through the roof window, the colour takes on a pale greenish hue, and in the evening it darkens to a much darker grey-green and feels warm and enveloping. Lighter touches, such as the white metal bed and arts-and-crafts painted chair, give fresh, light touches in contrast to the darker background.

You are allowed to disturb the peace of low-key natural shades and textures with a blast of nature-inspired colour, whether it's a fabulous floral fabric or something fresh and green and colourful from a flower stall, garden, or walk in the country

I go to houses where beautifully thought-out schemes in shades of Duck Egg, Mouse's Back and String are sacrificed to an overkill of harsh downlighting with the effect being more detention centre than cosy domestic space. Pools of light from lamps are more restful and create depths of light and shade. Cream-coloured paper shades are great for casting a warm yellow light.

Nature colours on the walls and scented green geraniums for a peaceful work retreat at Ett Hem, Stockholm

Supplies

Of sea, sky and hyacinths

Wall in Parma Gray, Farrow &Ball

Ticking fabric, Ian Mankin

Wall print designed by Ben Kendrick

Paper covered folder, Antica Legatoria Piazzesi Venezia.

Headboard in hand printed cotton, C & C Milano

Wall in Arsenic emulsion, Farrow & Ball

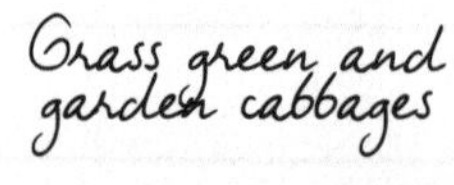

Wall in Teresa's Green emulsion, Farrow & Ball

Wall in Nancy's Blushes emulsion, Farrow & Ball

Background in Liberty tana lawn; chair painted in Tarragon Glory, Dulux

Location house, Chaucer Road, www.lightlocations.com.
Wall in 30GY/23/232 emulsion, Dulux

Wall in Citrine emulsion, Littlegreene; chairs in Powder Blue eggshell, Farrow & Ball

Daisy wallpaper, Art of Wallpaper; wall in Yellowcake emulsion, Farrow & Ball

Saffron, quince and summer beaches

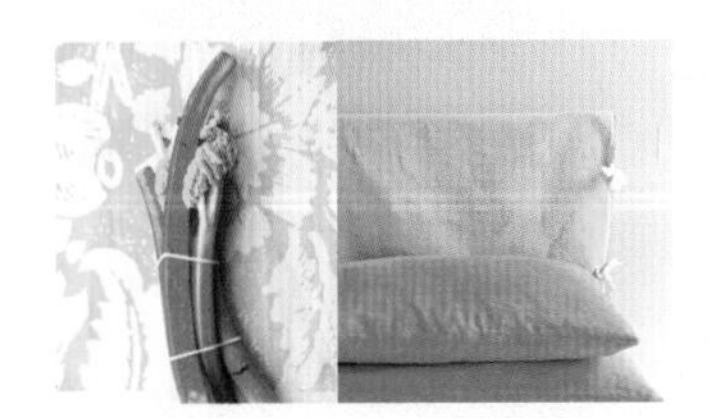

Yellow printed linen, Bennison fabrics; Bedhead in Fiona linen/cotton, Manuel Canovas

Cushion in Norma, Prune, linen, Manuel Canovas

Wall in Dayroom Yellow emulsion, Farrow & Ball

Left wall in Parma Gray emulsion, door in Babouschka eggshell, wall in Plummett emulsion, all by Farrow & Ball

Wall in Orange Aurora emulsion, Fired Earth

Lipstick and pink petals

Wall in Nancy's Blushes emulsion, Farrow & Ball

Curtains in Foch, rose cotton velvet, Manuel Canovas; Bowwood wallpaper, Colefax and Fowler

Wall in Cochineal emulsion, Fired Earth

Linen, hemp and cloud colours

Walls and door in Pigeon emulsion, Farrow & Ball

Cushion in Carla Safran linen/viscose, Manuel Canovas

Lamp 084, Studioilse, Wastberg

Places to go for inspiration

Herne Hill , Railton Road, Herne Hill, London, SE24 0JN
www.weareccfm.com/HerneHill
Everything from seasonal fruit and veg to beautiful dyed blankets and secondhand kitchenware

Brixton Farmers Market, Station Road, Brixton, London, SW9 8PA www.lfm.org.uk
9am–2pm every Sunday; plump cabbages, bags of freshly picked salad leaves and biodynamic eggs

Sunbury Antiques Market, Kempton Park Race Course, Staines Road East, Sunbury-on-Thames, Middlesex, TW16 5AQ
www.sunburyantiques.com
Vintage fabrics, white china, old bone handled cutlery

Dulwich Picture Gallery, Gallery Road, London, SE21 7AD
www.dulwichpicturegallery.org.uk

Skansen, Stiftelsen Skansen, Box 27807, 11593 Stockholm, 08-442 80 00
www.skansen.se
Open air museum of Swedish vernacular architecture spanning five centuries

Alcazar, Seville, Spain
www.alcazarsevilla.org
Moorish palace and gardens with, azjuleos tiles and rich Andalucian colours

Brockwell lido, Dulwich Road, London, SE24 0PA
www.fusion-lifestyle.com
Thirties lido and year long outdoor swimming at the 'Brixton Beach'

Monet's House at Giverny, 84 Rue Claude Monet, 27620 Giverny, France
www.giverny.org

Soane Museum
13 Lincoln's Inn Fields, London, WC2A 3BP
www.soane.org

Garden places

Sissinghurst
Biddenden Road, near Cranbrook, Kent, TN17 2AB
www.nationaltrust.org.uk
White garden designed by Vita Sackville West in the 1930s

Lytes Cary Manor
near Somerton, Somerset, TA11 7HU
www.nationaltrust.org.uk
Manor house and community garden

Petersham Nurseries
Petersham Road, Richmond, Surrey, TW10 7AG www.petershamnurseries.com
Rambling glasshouses are backdrop for plants and great food

Rosendal www.rosendalstradgard.se
Stiftelsen Rosendals Trädgård
Rosendalsterrassen 12
SE-115 21 STOCKHOLM, Sweden
Biodynamic garden with apple trees, roses, and bakery

Hauser & Wirth
Durslade Farm, Dropping Lane, Bruton, Somerset BA10 0NL
www.hauserwirthsomerset.com
Restored farm buildings for smart London gallery offshoot and garden by Piet Oudolf

Places to stay

Convento www.conventoolhao.com
White and airy bedrooms and a stunning rooftop terrace with views across the sea. Filipe and Eleanor also have more white rooms and houses to rent at
White terraces www.whiteterraces.com

Casa da luz, Olhão www.ocasadaluz.com
Beautifully restored white townhouse available to rent to lovely people.

Ett Hem Sköldungagatan 2
SE-114 27 Stockholm, Sweden
www.etthem.se
A home from home with 12 luxurious rooms, peace, blazing fires and homemade cake

Paint

Earthborn www.earthbornpaints.co.uk
Paint with natural matt textures

Fired Earth www.firedearth.com
Good range of colours, including 'Cochineal' a rich pink red (see Red chapter)

Cuprinol www.cuprinol.co.uk
Waterbased colours for outside: willow, a sludgy green, is my favourite

Farrow & Ball www.farrow-ball.com

Little Greene www.littlegreene.com

Annie Sloane www.anniesloan.co.uk
Chalk paints for furniture and walls

Dulux www.dulux.co.uk

Francesca's Paints
www.francescaspaint.com
Beautiful range of colours in limewash

Mylands www.mylands.co.uk

Paint Library www.paint-library.co.uk

Johnstons www.johnstonestrade.com
White Flortred floor paint

Online inspiration

Wallpapers

The Art of Wallpaper
www.theartofwallpaper.com
Hand screen printed designs

Colefax and Fowler www.colefax.com
Classic English country garden florals

Mini Moderns www.minimoderns.com
Wallpapers with a retro feel

Sanderson www.sanderson-uk.com
Good for stripes

Neisha Crosland www.neishacrosland.com
Wallpaper in geometrics and florals

Purestyle Borders www.purestyleonline.com
My range of wallpaper borders in collaboration with Fiona de Courcy Wheeler, in eight colourways

Fabrics

Manuel Canovas
www.manuelcanovas.com
Fabulous colours in plains and patterns

Bluebell gray www.bluebellgray.com

St Judes www.stjudesfabrics.co.uk

ROMO www.romo.com

Olicana www.olicana.co.uk

Liberty www.liberty.co.uk

Mark Alexander www.markalexander.com

Miss Print www.missprint.co.uk

Villa Nova www.villanova.co.uk

Pierre Frey www.pierrefrey.com

C&C Milano www.cec-milano.com

Osborne & Little
www.osborneandlittle.com

Shiela Coombes www.brian-yates.co.uk

Ian Mankin www.ianmankin.co.uk
The best source for blue and white striped cotton tickings

Designers Guild
www.designersguild.com
Fabulous colours

Bennison fabrics
www.bennisonfabrics.com
Beautiful printed linens

MacCulloch & Wallis
www.macculloch-wallis.co.uk
Cotton ginghams and sewing supplies

Les Indiennes www.lesindiennes.com
Handblocked prints

Household
Labour and Wait
www.labourandwait.co.uk
Timeless, functional products, such as watering cans, garden trugs, leather work gloves, pans, aprons and scrubbing brushes

John Lewis www.johnlewis.com
Everything from wool blankets and linen sheets to white plates and cutlery

Melin Tregwynt www.melintregwynt.co.uk
Woven blankets from Wales

TG Green www.tggreen.co.uk
Blue and white striped 20s-style Cornishware mugs, plates and bowls

Volga linen www.volgalinen.co.uk
Linen sheets and tablecloths

ANTA www.anta.co.uk
Tartan for ceramics

Hammam towels
www.hammamas.com
Lightweight towels from the Turkish hamman

Falcon enamelware
www.falconenamelware.com
New look for blue and white enamelware

Habibi www.habibi-interiors.com
Moroccan tiles

The Foodie Bugle
www.thefoodiebugleshop.com
Everything from linen teatowels to vintage tea cups

Mason Cash www.masoncash.co.uk
Cream coloured traditional pudding basins

Robert Welch www.robertwelch.com
Classic tableware

Wastberg www.wastberg.com
Lamp w084 by Studioilse

Antica Legatoria Piazzesi Venzia
www.legatoriapiazzesi.it
Handprinted paper stationery

Garden
National Society of Allotment and Leisure Gardeners Ltd
www.nsalg.org.uk
All about allotment gardening

Assocation Kokopelli Organic Seeds
www.organicseedsonline.com
Over 2,500 varieties of organic seeds

Brockwell Park Community greenhouses
www.brockwellparkcommunitygreenhouses.org.uk
Chillis and other seeds

Crocus www.crocus.co.uk
Great online resource; tulip bulbs – including white parrot tulips and raspberry rippled striped 'Triumph' tulips

David Austin www.davidaustinroses.com
900 varieties. My favourite pink and scented ones are Constance Spry; John Clare; Eglantine. White, scented and good in shade: Madame Alfred Carriere and New dawn. For rosehip syrup and jellies: Francie E Lester, shrub Rosa rugosa and Rosa rugosa 'Alba'.

Cottage Garden Plants
www.rosecottageplants.co.uk
Good range of alliums 'Christophii' and 'Gladiator' huge pompom flower heads

Fallen Fruit www.fallenfruit.org
Finding fruit in the city

Habitaid www.habitaid.co.uk
Native plants and seeds, classic apple varieties

Iron Art www.ironart.co.uk
Romantic garden arches in metal mesh

De Jager www.dejager.co.uk
Good for tulips

Organic gardening catalogue
www.organiccatalog.com
Organic composts and fertilizer

The Real Seed Cataloguen
www.realseeds.co.uk
Heirloom and non-hybrid seeds

Thompson & Morgan
www.thompson-morgan.com
Garden supplies, beans, peas and other seeds

Urban Bees www.urbanbees.co.uk
Bringing beekeeping to the city

Shepherds huts
www.plankbridge.com
Made to order huts on wheels for a new take on the home office or garden shed

More online inspiration for colouring life

www.remodelista.com

www.thechromologist.com

www.designsponge.com

www.decor8.com

www.kinfolk.com

www.pantone.com

www.thatsnotmyage.blogspot.co.uk

www.thewomensroomblog.co.uk

www.gardenista.com

www.pantone.com

www.dezeen.com

Index

For Tom, Georgie and Gracie

Thank you

Thank you to everyone who has helped make this beautiful book

Polly Powell
Amy Christian
Zoë Anspach
Krissy Mallett
And everyone at Pavilion

Vanessa Courtier – we are a great team!
Elsie Abdy Collins – brilliant assisting

Sources of huge inspiration
Piers de Laszlo
Filipe Monteiro and Eleanor Lefebure
Antonia Williams
Kevin and Frances Gould
Shelagh Sartin
Emma and Damon Heath
Sarah and Nick Langridge
Jo Tyler
Mandy Bonnell
Ilse and Oscar Pena
Katrin Cargill
Clare Conville
Fiona de Courcy Wheeler
Simon de Courcy Wheeler for photograph on page 198
Rachel Whiting for photographs on pages 39 and 100

...and from Vanessa

Zoë and Amy at Pavilion – thank you

Jane – always a great team!

Luke and Lizzy
David